HOW TO PUBLISH A BOOK FROM PRISON

ELIJAH R. FREEMAN

URBAN AINT DEAD

URBAN AINT DEAD
P.O Box 448
Maybrook, NY 12543

Cover Design: P. Wise / The Wise Services

Edited By: Veronica Rena Miller / Red Diamond Editing by V. Rena, LLC / reddiamondediting5@yahoo.com

URBAN AINT DEAD and coinciding logo(s) are registered properties.

Contact Author on FB: Elijah R. Freeman / IG: @the_future_of_urban_fiction

Contact Publisher at www.urbanaintdead.com

Email: urbanaintdead@gmail.com

Print ISBN: 979-8-9902387-8-7

CONTENTS

Soundtracks

Scan the QR Code below to listen to the Soundtracks/Singles
of some of your favorite U.A.D titles:

Don't have Spotify or Apple Music?
No Sweat!
Visit your choice streaming platform and search URBAN
AINT DEAD.

Currently on lock serving a bid?
JPay, iHeartRadio, WHATEVER!
We got you covered.

Simply log into your facility's kiosk or tablet, go to music and
search URBAN AINT DEAD.

URBAN AINT DEAD

Like & Follow us on social media:
FB - URBAN AINT DEAD
IG: @urbanaintdead
Tik Tok - @urbanaintdead

Submissions

Submit the first three chapters of your completed manuscript to urbanaintdead@gmail.com, subject line: Your book's title. The manuscript must be in a .doc file and sent as an attachment. The document should be in Times New Roman, double-spaced, and in size 12 font. Also, provide your synopsis and full contact information. If sending multiple submissions, they must each be in a separate email. Have a story but no way to submit it electronically? You can still submit to URBAN AINT DEAD. Send in the first three chapters, written or typed, of your completed manuscript to:

URBAN AINT DEAD
P.O Box 448
Maybrook, NY 12543

DO NOT send original manuscript. Must be a duplicate.
Provide your synopsis and a cover letter containing your full contact information.
Thanks for considering URBAN AINT DEAD.

PREFACE

"The walls of a prison are designed not only to keep the prisoners in but to keep the rest of society from knowing what is going on inside. Prison literature is very subversive in that it reaches out from inside the prison to the larger society. This is different literature and separate from what people consider modern American literature, but it is extremely important."

H. Bruce Franklin
author of Prison Literature in America

INTRODUCTION

Introduction By Kwame "Dutch" Teague

Doing time is an uphill battle. We encounter mountainous obstacles daily to merely maintain our sanity. So if you are one of the chosen few who can not only SURVIVE in this environment, but THRIVE in this environment, then I salute you. Especially if you are undertaking the mountainous task of publishing a book from behind the wall. People are going to doubt you, people are going to hate on you, and some may even try to stop you. But this is where *the real* gets separated from the fake, the sugar from the shaft, those who are not only committed but disciplined enough to execute a plan. Every step of the way you're going to face obstacles, big and small. From who's going to type it, to who's going to publish and promote it, but it can be done and my Lil Brah Elijah is going to show you how. Believe me, I have nothing but respect and admiration for this Brother because he is not only putting himself on, he's putting on a whole team and now he's putting *you* on! His words are jewels, don't waste them. And remember, just because something says IMPOS-SIBLE, there's two ways to read that one word! Peace!

Dutch author of the Dutch trilogy and the producer of the Dutch series on BET.

FOREWORD

Writing a book is a powerful way to connect with others, express yourself, and share your story, your knowledge, and your experiences with the world. In prison, writing can be a lifeline, a way to escape the confines of your cell and connect with people beyond the wall. Whether you're writing for yourself or for others, the act of putting pen to paper can be incredibly therapeutic, helping you to process your thoughts and emotions and gain a deeper understanding of yourself.

However, publishing a book from prison can be a daunting task. You may feel like the system is stacked against you, but with the right attitude, tools, and resources, it's possible to pull it off and make a meaningful impact. In this book, I will guide you through the process of publishing a book from prison, providing you with the practical tips and insights you need to succeed.

Getting started, the first step in publishing a book from prison is to _write it_. Urban Fiction, Urban Romance, and Street Lit are popular genres that cater to a specific audience. To begin, think about your experiences and the stories that you want to share. What unique perspective do you bring to the table? What sets your story apart from others? Once you have an idea, start writing. And while there are many other literary genres that the information in this book can be applied to, I will be shining a light on the **Urban** genre. In my journey as an author/publisher, I found that there aren't many books that touch on Urban Fiction and Street Lit, mostly because these genres, "our" genres, a lot of time aren't respected by the publishing industry.

Prison lit, street lit, or urban fiction emerged 50 years ago, but some historians would argue that it has roots in the 19th century.

"What we are calling *prison literature* is also what was coming out of the plantations right after Reconstruction," said H. Bruce Franklin, author of *Prison Literature in America*. "With mass incarceration in the late 1960s and 1970s, black prisoners began to connect their experiences to slavery," Franklin said. Donald Goines — a street hustler who began writing about his experiences while incarcerated — defined the modern genre, but it was then and in some ways remains invisible to the arbiters of American culture.

We aren't taken serious as writers. Why? Some would say because of subpar writing in an oversaturated industry, others would argue that it is directly related to the fact that these genres cater to black people. Nevertheless, much like Hip-hop and rap music, Urban Fiction is alive and well, and this truth was the inspiration behind the name of my company.

Despite the challenges faced by Urban Fiction and Street Lit authors, it's important to recognize the significance of these genres. They provide a platform for underrepresented voices and bring attention to issues that are often ignored in mainstream literature. By embracing and supporting these genres, we can help create a more inclusive publishing industry. As the saying goes, "If you don't see the book you want on the shelf, write it yourself." That said, let's continue to write and share our stories.

As I conclude this foreword, it must be said that the lack of representation and respect for Urban Fiction and Street Lit in the publishing industry should not discourage aspiring authors from pursuing their dreams. With the right knowledge, anyone can learn how to publish a book from prison or any other circumstance. Remember, the power of storytelling is not limited to a specific genre or race. As we continue on this journey, let us strive to create opportunities for ourselves and others.

Regardless of the reasons why Urban Fiction and Street Lit are often disregarded, it's important that we as writers and publishers continue to push for the recognition and respect that these genres deserve. This book isn't just about publishing books from prison. It's about breaking down barriers and making our voices heard. It's about using our experiences and perspectives to create compelling stories that can resonate with readers from all walks of life. So let's keep writing, keep publishing, and keep fighting for our place in the literary world.

URBAN AINT DEAD!

Finding Your Voice

"No one else in the wide world, since the dawn of time, has ever seen the world as you do, or can explain it as you can. This is what you have to offer that no one else can."
Edith Layton, The Crimson Crown

The first step to publishing a book from prison is ***finding your unique voice.*** Writing is a powerful tool for self-expression, and it's important to discover what you want to say and how you want to say it. This chapter will guide you through the process of finding your voice and developing your writing skills.

As an author, finding your voice is crucial to your success.

Your voice is what sets you apart from other writers and makes your work unique. When publishing, finding your voice can be especially challenging. However, with the right approach and mindset, it's possible to discover and develop your voice as an author. The two most effective ways to become a better author are to read and write vigorously!

Avid readers always turn out to be some of the best writers.

For me, starting out, I had no guidance as far as writing goes. All the skill that I applied was from the different books I read. I paid attention to how Eric Jerome Dickey used sentence variation to keep his readers enthralled. I peeped how Ashley Antoinette's (one half of the Ashley & Jaquavis duo) characters often had introspective outlooks that she used to finesse the reader into relating, therefore, caring about the character's outcome. I also paid attention to patterns in majority of the stories I read. Noticing a trend, I wrote with every intention on distinguishing my tales from the average. I wanted to be different, naturally, but I came to find out that this should be every writer's goal: to find their own voice.

I say this a lot so this may not be the last time I mention it in this book, but there are a lot of similarities between the music and publishing industry. Now, a lot of this new music sounds the same for the most part these days because all this auto tuning going on, but just as rappers have their own sound, so do authors. Snoop Dogg don't rap like YG, 21

Savage don't rap like Young Thug, and A$AP Rocky don't rap like Pop Smoke.

Make no mistake, not one author tells a story the same as another. You could give seven authors the same plotline and they would deliver seven different stories. And this, my fellow writers, is the beauty of storytelling. It's not so much the plot that mesmerizes – no, it's the storyteller. It's the voice that echoes off the pages and resonates within your soul. The way Zane weaves sensuality into her prose or how Sister Souljah instills a sense of rebellion and resistance, painting her words with the stark colors of reality. Each voice unique, each voice powerful.

The same as rappers, authors also have influences. You might find a bit of the late, great E. Lynn Harris in my dialogue, a sprinkle of Terry McMillan's wit in my humor, or a dash of Walter Mosley's suspense in my plot twists. But at the end of the day, my stories are mine. They're told with *my* voice, through the lens of *my* experiences. This isn't just a suggestion, it's a *necessity*.

Now, don't get me wrong. It's okay to draw inspiration from other authors. Hell, it's even encouraged. But don't get it twisted; there's a fine line between inspiration and imitation. You gotta learn to take the essence of what you admire about their style and make it your own, not just copy and paste. This ain't no paint-by-numbers game, this is art.

So, how do you find your voice? Well, it's a journey, not a destination. Your voice will evolve as you do, growing stronger and more distinct with each story you tell. And it all starts with self-reflection. Get to know yourself, your experiences, your perspectives, and let that seep into your writing. Your voice isn't something you find, it's something you *unleash*.

Just like how a rapper can't rap without a beat, an author can't write without a voice. It's the rhythm, the flow, the melody of your story. It's what makes your readers bob their heads, what makes them *feel* the words. It's the beat to your lyrical prose.

In the words of the iconic urban fiction author, K'wan Foye: "Your voice as an author is your fingerprint. It's unique, it's you. Don't try to suppress it. Embrace it, own it, and let it echo through the pages. That's how you leave a mark in the world of stories."

Understanding Your Purpose

Understanding your purpose is a good way to help you find your voice as an author. Why do you want to write a book? What message do you want to convey to your readers? By understanding your purpose, you can develop a clear vision for your book and your voice. This may very well be the most critical step in finding your voice. Your purpose is the reason why you are writing your book. It is the message that you want to convey to your readers, and it is what will give your book meaning and value.

I'm writing this book to inform those of you behind the wall who, like me years ago, was just trying to figure this thing out. But when I wrote *Triggadale*: *Shots Fired,* I was tired of telling my bunkmates about an era in my city during the early 2000's when the crunk music wave was the hype and young aspiring rap groups looking to be the next *Crime Mob* were beefing amongst each other. I wanted to get that story out of my system and be done with it once and for all. It was a time long ago that no one talked about, but the people who lived it or witnessed one of the street wars by chance. Fresh in the system, I was hearing about guys from my hood who had been locked up since then as a result of that beef. With the gang wave hitting Georgia heavy around 2009 – 2010, the throwbacks cliques had become a thing of the past. I wanted to be the one to highlight that era. I had to get it out to move on. The characters were talking in my head. The memories were burning to be set free. It was personal. I got it done. So whether you want to inform on a subject matter, you want to tell your story, you feel inspired to write about characters based on the dead homies so that they forever live through your pen, or if you want to write about the down ass bitch you loved but let get away, pimp yo pen!

All I'm saying is *your purpose* should be the driving force behind your writing. It should be something that you are passionate about and that you believe in. It should be something that you are willing to put in the time and effort to achieve, because I ain't gone hold you, the pay in the beginning ain't gone be hittin' on nothin'! A lot of people come into the publishing industry with unrealistic expectations. They figure they'll put out a book and make millions overnight.

Newsflash: My first royalty check was for one hundred and something dollars, and that was only because a lot of friends and family supported my first release. The second and third royalty checks weren't even that much, and there were months I barely made anything at all. My purpose kept me going.

Lockdown Publication C.E.O CA$H said, *"New authors, if you're a pretty good writer and you're fully committed to it, you'll eventually break through. If you don't, either you're not as good of a writer as you thought or you're not as committed as it takes."*

Here are some questions to ask yourself to help you understand your purpose:

1. Why do you want to write a book?

Your reason for writing a book may be personal, such as documenting your life story or sharing your experiences with others. Or it may be to educate, inspire, or entertain your readers. Whatever your reason, it is essential to understand why you want to write a book.

2. What message do you want to convey to your readers?

Your message is the heart of your book. It is what you want your readers to take away from your writing. It may be a message of hope, resilience, or perseverance. It may be a message of warning, caution, or advice. Whatever your message, it should be clear, concise, and impactful.

3. Who is your target audience?

Your target audience is the group of people who will be most interested in reading your book. It may be people who have gone through similar experiences as you, or it may be a broader audience interested in your genre. For example, my target audience for this book is incarcerated aspiring authors. Understanding your target audience will help you tailor your writing to their needs and interests. For instance, Street Lit readers may want emphasis on the beef in a story while romance readers crave emphasis on the relationship in the plotline. Erotica readers may feign for the sex scenes in a book while Christian fiction readers may DNF (do not finish) a book for being too graphic. **DO NOT** be the "green as White House grass" author who thinks their book is for everyone. I can assure you it's not.

4. What do you hope to achieve with your writing?

Your goals for your writing may be personal, such as gaining closure or healing, or they may be more significant, such as making a difference in the world. Understanding your goals will help you stay focused and motivated throughout the writing process.

In addition to understanding your purpose, there are

some other things to consider when finding your voice as an author. These include:

1. **Your writing style.**

Your writing style is the way you write. It is your unique voice and personality that comes through in your writing. It may be formal or informal, humorous or serious, and so on. Your writing style should be authentic and reflect your personality and voice.

2. **Your genre.**

Your genre is the category or type of book you are writing. It may be fiction or non-fiction, romance, mystery, or science fiction, among others. Choosing the right genre for your book is essential as it will help you reach your target audience.

3. **Your tone.**

Your tone is the mood or attitude that comes through in your writing. It may be serious, humorous, sarcastic, or optimistic, among others. Your tone should be consistent throughout your book and reflect your purpose and message.

4. **Your structure.**

Your structure is the way you organize your book. It may be chronological, thematic, or a combination of both. Choosing the right structure for your book is essential, as it will help you convey your purpose and message effectively.

5. **Your point of view.**

Your point of view is the perspective from which you tell your story. It may be first-person, second-person, or third-person. Choosing the right point of view for your book is essential, as it will help you connect with your readers and convey your purpose and message effectively.

Once you have a clear understanding of your purpose, writing style, genre, tone, structure, and point of view, you can begin to develop your voice as an author.

Developing Your Voice

Your voice is your unique style and personality that comes through in your writing. It is what makes your writing stand out and connect with your readers. Developing your voice as an author takes time and practice, but it is essential to creating a successful book.

Here are some tips to help you develop your voice:

1. **Read widely.**

Reading is one of the best ways to develop your writing skills and voice. Read books in your genre and outside your genre to gain a broader perspective and develop your writing skills. Voracious reading can help you discover what you like and what you don't like, and it can inspire you to try new things.

2. **Practice writing.**

The more you write, the better you will become at it. Practice writing every day, even if it is just for a few minutes. Set aside time to write and stick to it. So, write regularly. The more you write, the more you'll develop your voice as an author.

3. Write authentically.

Write in your own voice and style. Be true to yourself and write from your heart. Your writing should reflect your personality, beliefs, and values. Writing honestly and authentically can help you connect with your readers and create a deeper emotional impact.

4. Experiment with different styles and techniques.

Try different writing styles and techniques to find what works best for you. Experiment with different tones, structures, and points of view to find your unique voice.

5. Seek feedback.

Feedback is essential to improving your writing skills and developing your voice. Find someone you trust to give you honest feedback on your writing. Listen to their feedback and use it to improve your writing. Make sure it's someone qualified. Homeboys, random guys around the dorm, and family don't count. These are people that are subject to tell you you're good to either make you feel good about your writing or because they actually think it is. The problem with that is these people could be mistaken. Giving you false hope hurts more than helps. Then when you send it to someone who is qualified, you think they're hating on you or don't want to see you make it. No. Get a *qualified* opinion from the jump. Don't be afraid to challenge yourself and be open to suggestions. No matter how good you are or think you are as a writer, there's always room for improvement. Writing is a never ending journey. The moment you think you can no longer grow in your craft is the day you need to park yo pen.

In essence, knowing your purpose is a key steppingstone to finding your voice as a writer. It's the engine that fuels your narrative and gives it meaning. Your purpose extends beyond the pages of your book; it impacts your readers and resonates with their own experiences. With clarity in purpose, you can weave stories that not only entertain but also inspire, educate, and provoke thought.

Your purpose isn't necessarily about achieving fame or fortune but about creating a connection with your readers. It's about giving a voice to the silent stories within you, influencing perspectives, and creating a lasting impact. This understanding helps shape your unique writing style and voice – the signature that sets your work apart.

In the words of incarcerated author Mike Enemigo, "Your purpose is your internal compass. It guides your narrative, giving it direction and depth. It's not just about telling a story; it's about sharing a piece of your world. When you write with purpose, your words carry weight and your voice echoes far beyond the confines of your current circumstance." Therefore, identify your purpose, write with conviction, and let your voice resonate.

. . .

Here are some additional tips and information on understanding your purpose and developing your voice as an author:

1. **Write for your audience.**

"When I discovered my audience, I began to curate my characters voices through that lens," Nai, author of the Thug Me The Right Way series says. *"As a romantic and product of the hood, I write stories of Black love in all its many facets. I coined myself* The Hood Love Dealer *because of my unique way of storytelling that takes you on the journey with my book baes and the women who love and adore them.*

Understanding your target audience is key to developing your voice as an author. Consider the age, gender, interests, and values of your readers when writing your book. Use language and examples that will resonate with them and help them connect with your message.

2. **Be specific.**

When developing your purpose and message, be specific and focused. Avoid vague or general statements and instead, hone in on the specific idea or theme you want to convey. This will help keep your writing clear and concise and make your message more impactful.

3. **Use your own experiences.**

One way to develop your voice as an author is to draw from your own experiences. Share your personal stories and insights to make your writing more relatable and authentic. This can help readers connect with you on a deeper level and make your message more impactful. This will make your voice as an author unique.

4. Find inspiration.

Inspiration can come from many sources, including books, movies, music, and art. Find what inspires you and use it to fuel your writing. Whether it's a particular genre, author, or artist, use their work as a guide and inspiration for your own writing.

5. Edit and revise.

Editing and revising are essential parts of the writing process. Once you have a first draft, go back and read it with a critical eye. Look for areas where you can improve your writing, such as sentence structure, grammar, and pacing. Revise your work until you are satisfied with the final product. For the best results, set it aside two weeks to a month while you work on something else. Then pull it back out and go over it again with fresh eyes. You'll be surprised how many errors you find after swearing you went through it thoroughly. Thank me later.

6. Stay motivated.

Writing a book is a challenging and time-consuming process, but it can also be incredibly rewarding. To stay motivated, set achievable goals and track your progress. Celebrate your successes along the way, and don't be too hard on yourself if you experience setbacks. Remember, writing is a journey, not a destination.

In conclusion, understanding your purpose and developing your voice as an author are essential steps to creating a successful book. By writing for your audience, being specific, using your own experiences, finding inspiration, editing and revising, and staying motivated, you can create a book that resonates with readers and makes a meaningful impact.

Discovering Your Unique Perspective

Every writer has a unique perspective, shaped by their experiences, background, and worldview. As a prisoner, *your perspective* is especially valuable and important. In this chapter, we'll explore how to tap into your unique perspective and use it to develop your voice as an author.

As stated before, prisoners have a perspective that is unlike anyone else's. Your experiences, background, and worldview have been shaped by your unique circumstances, and it is essential that you tap into this perspective when writing your book. *"I see the world through the eyes of a nigga behind the wall,"* I find myself saying a lot, and it's so true. Whether we realize it or want to speak on it or not, the way someone doing time views love, trust, relationships, danger, risks, losses, etc., is completely different from that of someone living in the free world and vice versa. No matter how many books they read, movies they watch, or people they know that tell them what prison is like, they will *NEVER* know what it's like to be locked away doing calendars. I can say that and stand on it because nothing I saw or heard could've prepared me for this lifestyle. That in mind, I began to wonder about other professions and walks of life. We have a general idea of what we think it's like to be a rapper, but we really don't know what they go through and I don't believe it's all good, either. The same is true for a nurse, janitor, teacher, and so on. We think we know, but in all actuality, we don't.

The beauty, or perhaps the tragedy, of life is that we are all shaped by our personal experiences. We don't just get to walk a mile in someone else's shoes. We live our own miles in our own shoes, and those miles shape how we see and understand the world around us. The unique trials and tribulations that I've undergone behind bars have carved a perspective on life that is mine alone. Yet, I realize that we all have our own battles, our own hardships that paint our worldview. Every profession, every walk of life, has its own unique set of experiences that outsiders can never fully comprehend. We may think we understand, but without actually living it, our understanding will always be incomplete. This realization led me to deeper introspection about my own journey and experiences. I like to dig deep and give my readers street specifics. Not just the general stuff that everyone talks, writes, and knows about.

For example: Everyone knows robbing, stealing, and killing goes on in the hood but what if I write a scene about three young niggas, where one has a dollar and two have two dollars apiece. They use the dollar to get a cigarillo and take the four dollars up the street to the weed man to see about getting a sack for the 4 ($4 for the ones who ain't street). That's the struggle and a personal experience of mine in my early teens. It's an I-can't-make-this-up moment. I live for those. I love to write them and read them. It's what separates the ones who simply write Urban Fiction/Street Lit and those who are either living it or have actually lived it. If your sitting in a cell, right now, reading this, you have plenty of these moments. I'm sure we can all agree that a lot of things we've witnessed, we wouldn't have imagined had we not been exposed to them.

One of the first steps in discovering your unique perspective is to reflect on your own experiences. What have you been through that others have not? How have your experiences shaped the way you see the world? What lessons have you learned that you can share with others?

As you journey deeper into your self-reflection, you'll find that your unique perspective isn't just about the experiences you've had but also about how you've processed and understood those experiences. This is a crucial element in developing your voice as an author. The same event can happen to two different people, but the way they interpret and express their experiences can be completely different. This is where your unique perspective comes into play.

Ask yourself: What emotions did I feel during my experiences? How did they change me? How did they shape my values? These questions can dig deeper into your psyche and might reveal some truths about your perspective that you may not have considered before.

One thing that many of us forget is that our perspective is not fixed. It changes and evolves as we grow and as we encounter new experiences. Even as a prisoner, your perspective can change. You may have entered the prison system with one mindset, but over time, through interactions with others, through reading, through personal introspection, and through living the experience of incarceration, your perspective may shift. This evolution of perspective is a rich source of material for your writing.

The most powerful and authentic stories often come from the author's own experiences. As someone writing from prison, you have a unique perspective that can add depth and realism to your Urban Fiction. Reflect on your experiences and emotions and consider how you can incorporate them into your writing in a meaningful and impactful way.

In addition to reflecting on your own experiences, consider the experiences of others around you. Everyone in prison has a unique story, a unique path that led them to where they are. You can learn from these stories, and they can help you to broaden your perspective. They can also provide a rich source of material for your writing.

Remember, your unique perspective is not a disadvantage; it is *a strength*. It is what sets you apart from other writers. It gives your writing an authenticity that can't be replicated. By tapping into this perspective, you'll be able to create compelling narratives that will resonate with your readers.

While it's important to be truthful to your experiences, it's also important to remember that you're writing for an audience. Think about what you want your readers to take away from your writing. What do you want them to feel? What do you want them to learn? By considering your audience's perspective, you can shape your writing in a way that will engage them, enlighten them, and perhaps even change their perspective.

For example, this book was written primarily with aspiring incarcerated men and women authors in mind, so it was important for me to use language and cultural references that were familiar to them. I can quote Edgar Allan Poe or Oliver Wendell Holmes, but for the most part, the audience I'm writing this for has nothing in common with those men. Therefore, it holds little to no weight, versus me quoting Wahida Clark, CA$H, or Dutch. Why? Because they have been successful at what the target audience purchased this book for. If you're reading this, you can relate to them, and they can relate to you and where you're going. Not to say all quotes in this book are or will be from Urban authors, but that's my goal for the most part because I want these pages to resonate with my readers, right now and for decades to come.

Notice I didn't say where you're "trying to go." That's because we're not "trying" anything. "Trying" is a noble way of admitting failure and with the tools provided in this book, you can't lose. All five people mentioned above have been successful pimpin' their pen behind the wall, and so will you if you stay down.

Finally, it is important to be authentic in your writing. Your unique perspective is what sets you apart as an author, and it is important that you stay true to yourself and your experiences. Don't try to imitate other writers or adopt a style that doesn't feel natural to you. Instead, focus on expressing your own voice and perspective in a genuine way.

Discovering your unique perspective isn't a one-time event, but rather a continuous process that evolves with you. It's an ongoing journey, one that's as unique as you are. So, embrace it, explore it, and most importantly, write it. Your voice matters, and the world needs to hear it.

Here are a few more tips and insights on discovering your unique perspective as an author:

1. **Embrace Your Experiences**: Your unique perspective is largely informed by your individual experiences. As a pris-

oner, you have access to a world that many people will never see or understand firsthand. This can be a powerful tool for creating compelling narratives, particularly in genres like Urban Fiction, Urban Romance, and Street Literature. Use your experiences to create vivid, authentic characters and settings. These experiences, while difficult, can provide a unique voice and viewpoint. Don't shy away from them. Instead, channel them into your writing. Many readers appreciate and seek out stories that provide fresh, distinctive perspectives, and your experiences could be the source of that.

2. **Reflect on Your Identity**: Your identity goes beyond being a prisoner. You may be a father, a son, an artist, a veteran, or many other things. Each aspect of your identity contributes to your unique perspective. Reflect on these roles and consider how they inform your views of the world. For example, how does being a father affect your views on love and sacrifice? How does your background or upbringing shape your understanding of street life? By exploring these questions, you can develop a deeper understanding of your unique perspective and how to express it in your writing.

3. **Engage with Diverse Narratives**: Reading broadly can help you understand and refine your own perspective. Explore works from writers of various backgrounds, in different genres, and from different periods. This can provide you with a broader understanding of the world and the people in it, which can inform your own writing. Again, it's

also beneficial to read works that reflect your own experiences and identity. Seeing how other writers have approached similar topics can provide inspiration and help you find new ways to express your unique perspective.

4. Practice Self-Reflection: Regularly taking the time to reflect on your thoughts, feelings, and reactions can help you understand your unique perspective. Journaling can be a particularly effective tool for this. By writing regularly about your experiences and thoughts, you can gain a better understanding of your own perspective and how it influences your writing. This can also help you identify recurring themes or ideas in your thoughts, which can provide a starting point for exploring your unique perspective in your writing.

5. Embracing Your Authenticity: Authenticity is about being true to who you are at your core. It's about acknowledging your strengths, accepting your weaknesses, and living in a way that aligns with your values and beliefs. As a writer, embracing your authenticity means telling the stories that matter to you, in a way that reflects your unique perspective and voice. This isn't always easy, but it's essential for creating work that is genuine, compelling, and true to who you are. Remember, your authenticity is your superpower; it's what sets you apart and makes your voice unforgettable to your readers.

Embracing Your Authenticity

I don't listen to fake rappers and I don't read fake Urban Fiction authors!!

-Me

Authenticity is key to developing a strong voice as an author. When writing from prison, it can be tempting to try to fit into a particular mold or cater to a certain audience. You may feel pressure to conform to certain expectations or to write what you think people want to read. However, the key to developing a strong voice as an author is to embrace your authenticity and write from a place of truth and honesty. In this chapter, we'll explore how to tap into your authenticity and use it to strengthen your voice.

What Does Authenticity Mean?

Authenticity is a term that gets thrown around a lot, but what does it actually mean? At its core, authenticity is about being true to who you are. It's about acknowledging your strengths and weaknesses, your experiences, and your values, and using them to guide your decisions and actions.

When it comes to writing, authenticity means tapping into your unique perspective and using that perspective to shape your voice and your message. It means being honest about your experiences and writing from a place of truth, even if it's difficult or uncomfortable.

. . .

Why Authenticity Matters?

In the world of publishing, *authenticity* is key. Readers can tell when a writer is being insincere or trying to pander to a particular audience. When you write from a place of authenticity, your readers will be able to sense your sincerity and connect with your message on a deeper level.

Additionally, embracing your authenticity can help you stand out in a crowded market. There are countless writers out there, but no one has had the same experiences as you or sees the world in exactly the same way. By tapping into your unique perspective and writing from a place of truth, you can create a voice and a message that is completely your own.

How to Embrace Your Authenticity?

Embracing your authenticity isn't always easy, especially when you're writing from prison. However, there are a few things you can do to tap into your unique perspective and use it to strengthen your voice.

1. Reflect on Your Life.

One of the best ways to tap into your authenticity (as we mentioned in the previous section) is to reflect on your life and experiences. Take some time to think about the events and people that have shaped you, both positively and negatively. Consider how your experiences have shaped your values, beliefs, and worldview.

As you reflect on your life, ask yourself the following questions:

- What are my strengths and weaknesses?
- What are my core values?
- What are my passions and interests?
- What do I want to communicate to the world through my writing?

By answering these questions honestly, you can start to tap into your unique perspective and use it to guide your writing.

2. **Write from the Heart.**

When you're writing from prison, it's easy to get bogged down in the details or to focus on what you think people want to hear. However, the key to writing authentically is to write from the heart. Write about what you know and what you're passionate about. Don't worry about whether it's "marketable" or "popular."

Instead, focus on telling your story in the most honest and compelling way possible. Write about the people and experiences that have shaped you, and don't be afraid to be vulnerable or emotional.

3. Be True to Your Voice.

Your voice is what makes your writing unique. It's the way you express yourself and the tone you use to convey your message. When you're writing from prison, it can be easy to try to mimic the voice of other writers or to adopt a particular style or tone because you think it will be more marketable. However, it's important to be true to *your own* voice and style. Don't try to be someone you're not or write in a way that doesn't feel natural to you.

Instead, embrace your unique voice and use it to convey your message in the most authentic way possible. Write in a way that feels true to who you are, and don't be afraid to experiment with different styles and tones until you find the one that feels right for you.

4. Don't Be Afraid to Take Risks.

Authenticity often requires taking risks and stepping outside of your comfort zone. When you're writing from prison, it can be tempting to play it safe and stick to what you know. However, taking risks can help you grow as a writer and tap into your authenticity in new and exciting ways.

This could mean experimenting with different genres or

writing styles or exploring topics that are outside of your usual comfort zone. I know this sounds contradictory to being true to your voice, but it's not. Don't be afraid to push the boundaries of what you think is possible, and don't let *fear* hold you back from expressing your true self.

5. Seek Feedback and Support.

Finally, seeking feedback and support from others can be a valuable way to tap into your authenticity and strengthen your voice as a writer. This could mean joining a writing group or workshop, working with a mentor or editor, or simply sharing your work with trusted friends and family members. I have to say this, though. Please, don't go off of what someone says and feel as though it's the end all be all. Keep an open mind to what the people whose opinion truly matter like your editor and your publisher (especially if you're in a traditional relationship). Traditional publishers can only make their money back if you sell copies. Meaning, it's in their best interest to see to it that they put you out at your best. If they're giving you advice, more times than not, it's sound and based off of experience. I don't think anyone gets in this business to lose money.

"As authors, we never stop growing," Thomas Habersham says. *"The moment we do, by thinking we've learned all we can learn, we may as well stop writing."*

Getting feedback from others can help you see your work

from a new perspective and identify areas where you can improve. It can also be a valuable source of support and encouragement as you navigate the challenges of writing from prison.

No Cap!!

Embracing your authenticity is essential for developing a strong voice as a writer, especially when you're writing from prison. By tapping into your unique perspective and writing from a place of truth and honesty, you can create a voice and a message that is completely your own. It may not always be easy, but the rewards of writing *authentically* are well worth the effort. So go ahead, embrace your authenticity and write from the heart.

Here are a few additional points to consider when it comes to embracing your authenticity as a writer:

1. **Authenticity is a process.**

Embracing your authenticity as a writer isn't something that happens overnight. It's a process that requires self-reflection, experimentation, and a willingness to take risks. It's okay to make mistakes and try new things as you work to find your voice and message. Remember, your authenticity is unique to you and it may take some time to fully tap into it

2. **Authenticity doesn't mean oversharing.**

While writing authentically means being honest and vulnerable, it doesn't mean you have to share everything about your personal life or experiences. You should feel comfortable setting boundaries and deciding what you're comfortable sharing with your readers. It's always important to protect your privacy and safety, especially if you're writing from prison. Watch out for R.I.C.O (if you know you know).

3. Authenticity can help you connect with your readers.

When you write from a place of authenticity, you're more likely to connect with your readers on a *deeper* level. This is because readers can sense when a writer is being genuine and sincere in their writing. By being honest about your experiences and emotions, you can create a connection with your readers that goes beyond just telling a story.

4. Authenticity can help you find your niche.

When you write authentically, you're more likely to attract readers who resonate with your message and voice. This can help you build a loyal following and find your niche in the publishing world. Remember, there's an audience out there for every type of writing, so don't be afraid to embrace your unique perspective and voice.

As I said before, embracing your authenticity as a writer is about being true to yourself and your experiences. By tapping into your unique perspective and writing from a place of truth and honesty, you can create a voice and message that is completely your own. It may not always be easy, but the rewards of writing authentically are well worth the effort.

. . .

Experimenting with Different Writing Styles

As an author, finding your voice is crucial to your success. Your **writing style** is an essential component of your voice, and it's what sets you apart from other writers. Experimenting with different writing styles can be an effective way to develop your voice as an author, and it can help you create a unique and engaging reading experience for your audience. There are many different writing styles and techniques you can use to develop your voice as an author. In this section, we'll explore some of the most common writing styles, such as narrative, descriptive, and persuasive writing, and provide you with tips for experimenting with different styles to find what works for you.

Narrative Writing

Narrative writing is a style of writing that tells a story. It typically involves a plot, characters, and a setting, and it can be either fictional or nonfictional. Narrative writing is often used in fiction, but it can also be used in memoirs, biographies, and other forms of nonfiction.

If you're interested in narrative writing, there are a few things you can do to experiment with this style. One way is to practice writing short stories. Short stories are an excellent way to develop your narrative skills because they allow you to focus on a single plot and a few characters. When writing a short story, focus on creating a compelling plot, developing your characters, and creating a setting that enhances the story's mood and tone.

Another way to experiment with narrative writing is to write a longer piece of fiction, such as a novel. Novels are more complex than short stories, and they require careful planning and organization. When writing a novel, focus on creating a well-developed plot, developing complex and interesting characters, and creating a world that feels real and immersive.

Descriptive Writing

Descriptive writing is a style of writing that uses language to create a vivid image in the reader's mind. It's often used in poetry, but it can also be used in prose. Descriptive writing is all about using sensory details to create a rich, immersive experience for the reader.

If you're interested in descriptive writing, one way to experiment with this style is to practice writing descriptive paragraphs. Descriptive paragraphs are short pieces of writing that focus on a single object, person, or scene. When writing a descriptive paragraph, focus on using sensory details such as sight, sound, smell, taste, and touch to create a vivid image in the reader's mind.

Another way to experiment with descriptive writing is to

try writing poetry. Poetry is an excellent form of descriptive writing because it allows you to use language in creative and unconventional ways. When writing poetry, focus on using vivid imagery, figurative language, and sound devices to create a rich and immersive experience for the reader.

Persuasive Writing

Persuasive writing is a style of writing that aims to persuade the reader to take a particular action or believe a particular idea. It's often used in advertising, journalism, and political speeches. Persuasive writing is all about using language to convince the reader that your point of view is *the right* one.

If you're interested in persuasive writing, one way to experiment with this style is to practice writing persuasive essays. Persuasive essays are pieces of writing that argue for or against a particular idea or position. When writing a persuasive essay, focus on presenting a clear and compelling argument, using evidence and logic to support your position, and anticipating and addressing counterarguments.

Another way to experiment with persuasive writing is to write an advertising copy. Advertising copy is a form of writing that aims to persuade the reader to take a particular action, such as buying a product or signing up for a service. When writing advertising copy, focus on creating a compelling message that appeals to the reader's needs and desires, using persuasive language and emotional appeals to convince the reader to take action.

Conclusion

Experimenting with different writing styles is an essential part of developing your voice as an author. Whether you're interested in narrative writing, descriptive writing, persuasive writing, or another style, there are many ways to explore and experiment with different techniques and approaches. Remember to be true to yourself and to write from your heart, and you'll find that your voice as an author will naturally emerge over time. With dedication, hard work, and a willingness to take risks, you can develop a unique and compelling voice as an author and share your stories with the world.

Here are some additional tips and considerations for experimenting with different writing styles:

1. **Practice, practice, practice.** The more you write in different styles, the more comfortable and confident you will become in using them.

2. **Read and analyze works by other authors who excel in the style you are interested in.** Take note of their techniques, language, and pacing, and try to incorporate what you learn into your own writing.

3. Don't be afraid to mix and match different styles. You don't need to stick to one style exclusively; in fact, using a combination of styles can create a more dynamic and engaging piece of writing.

4. Consider your audience. Some styles may be more appropriate or effective for certain types of readers or genres. For example, persuasive writing may be more effective in non-fiction or self-help books, while descriptive writing may be more effective in literary fiction.

5. Don't forget about editing and revision. Once you've experimented with different styles and techniques, it's important to revise and refine your work to ensure that it is clear, compelling, and effective.

Remember, finding your voice as an author is a process that takes time and practice. Don't be discouraged if it takes some trial and error to find the style that feels right for you. Keep experimenting, keep writing, and keep learning, and you'll be well on your way to developing a unique and powerful voice as an author.

Writing Your Manuscript

In the journey of writing your manuscript, the first step is to find your unique voice, which is explored in depth in the previous sections. Now, we will focus on the art of *crafting your manuscript.* Whether you are writing memoirs, fiction, or non-fiction, there are universal principles that can guide you. Here are some key points to help you write a manuscript that resonates with readers:

Organizing Your Ideas

1. **Brainstorm:** Allow yourself to freely generate ideas without any judgment or editing. Write down everything that comes to mind: characters, scenes, themes, dialogue, etc.

2. **Outline:** Create a rough sketch of your manuscript. It doesn't need to be detailed, but it should give a basic structure for your story. The outline should include the major events and turning points in your narrative.

3. **Develop Chapters:** Break down your story into manageable parts or chapters. Each chapter should have its own mini-arc contributing to the overall narrative.

4. **Use Visual Aids:** Mind maps, storyboards, or flowcharts can help you visualize the structure of your story and the relationships between characters or events.

Developing Your Characters

1. **Know Your Characters:** Understand your characters as if they were real people. What are their motivations, fears, dreams, and quirks?

2. **Show, Don't Tell:** Let readers discover your characters

through their actions and dialogues, rather than through explicit descriptions.

3. **Character Arcs:** Plan how your characters will evolve throughout the story. The best characters are dynamic, experiencing growth and transformation.

Creating a Compelling Narrative Arc

1. **Establish the Stakes:** Make sure it's clear what's at risk for your characters. Stakes increase tension and keep readers engaged.

2. **Conflict and Resolution:** Your story should have a central conflict that drives the narrative. The *climax* is the point of maximum tension or conflict, and the *resolution* is where the conflict is resolved.

3. **Pacing:** Balance action, dialogue, and description to maintain a steady narrative pace. Too much of one can slow down the story or disengage the reader.

Strategies for Improving Your Writing

1. **Write Regularly:** Establish a daily writing routine. This helps you stay committed and keeps your writing skills sharp.

2. **Read Widely:** Reading helps improve your writing. It gives you a sense of different styles, voices, and genres, and broadens your vocabulary.

3. **Revise:** Writing is rewriting. Don't be afraid to make changes. Editing and revising are essential parts of the process.

4. **Peer Review:** Get feedback from fellow inmates, friends, or family. They can provide valuable insights and spot areas you might have missed.

5. **Patience:** Writing a manuscript is a long process. Be patient with yourself and remember that every word you write brings you closer to your goal.

Remember, the key to a compelling manuscript is authenticity. Let your unique voice shine through every page, every chapter. This is *your* story, told in *your* words. Stay true to yourself, and readers will connect with your work.

It's time to start writing your manuscript. This can be a challenging and time-consuming process, but with the right approach, you can create a powerful and engaging book.

Identifying Your Writing Strengths and Weaknesses

As a writer, especially when writing urban fiction, it's essential to know *your strengths and weaknesses*. This self-awareness will help you to develop a unique voice that distinguishes you from other writers and keeps your readers engaged. The process of self-discovery can be a challenging one, but it is a necessary step towards becoming a successful author. In this section, we will guide you through different strategies for identifying your writing strengths and weaknesses and how to use this knowledge to write a compelling book from prison.

1. Reflect on Your Writing Experiences.

The first step in identifying your writing strengths and weaknesses is to reflect on your past writing experiences. Think about the pieces you've written before and consider the following questions:

- What topics did you enjoy writing about the most?
- What themes or issues do you feel most comfortable addressing?
- What aspects of your writing have you received the most positive feedback on?
- What parts of your writing have been criticized or suggested for improvement?

By answering these questions, you can start to identify patterns and trends in your writing that can help you understand your strengths and weaknesses.

2. Analyze Your Writing Style.

To develop your voice, it's important to analyze your

writing style. This includes the way you structure your sentences, your choice of vocabulary, and your use of dialogue. Consider the following questions:

- Do you prefer writing in short, punchy sentences or long, flowing ones?

- Is your vocabulary simple and straightforward or do you like to use more complex and obscure words?

- How do you approach writing dialogue?

- How do your characters interact with one another?

By understanding your writing style, you can begin to identify the elements that make your writing unique and authentic, as well as areas where you can improve.

3. Read Urban Fiction "AND" Other Genres.

Reading widely, especially within the urban fiction genre, can help you identify your own writing strengths and weaknesses. By exposing yourself to different writing styles and techniques, you can learn from other authors and gain insights into what works and what doesn't. As you read, take note of the following:

- What aspects of the writing do you enjoy and admire?

- What elements of the writing do you find off-putting or jarring?

- Which narrative devices or techniques do you think you

could incorporate into your own writing?

By becoming a *critical reader*, you can develop a better understanding of your own writing preferences and how they may align with, or diverge from, the conventions of urban fiction.

4. Seek Feedback from Others.

One of the most effective ways to identify your writing strengths and weaknesses is to seek feedback from others. This can include friends, family members, fellow inmates, or even prison staff who are willing to read your work and provide honest feedback. When soliciting feedback, consider asking the following questions:

- What aspects of the story or characters did the reader find most engaging?

- Were there any parts of the writing that were confusing or unclear?

- What suggestions does the reader have for improving the writing?

Remember to approach feedback with an open mind and be willing to accept constructive criticism. This feedback can help you pinpoint areas where you excel and areas where you can improve, ultimately strengthening your writing and voice.

5. Practice Writing Exercises.

Regular writing practice can help you identify your strengths and weaknesses as a writer. Set aside time each day or week to engage in writing exercises that challenge you to explore different aspects of writing, such as character development, dialogue, or world-building. By experimenting with different techniques and styles, you can gain a better understanding of your strengths and weaknesses.

There are several writing exercises you can try out, including:

A. **Writing prompts:** These are short writing exercises that provide a starting point for your writing, such as a sentence or a phrase. You can find writing prompts online or create your own. One of my personal favorites that I do often is randomly open a book, take that first sentence off the page within, write it at the top of a page of notebook paper, and freestyle a whole page of fiction off that one sentence. Go nonstop, no stopping until the entire page is filled.

B. **Character sketches:** This exercise involves creating detailed character profiles for your main characters, including their backstory, personality traits, and motivations.

C. **Dialogue practice:** Write a scene that involves two or more characters engaging in conversation. Try to make the dialogue sound natural and authentic.

D. **World-building:** Create a detailed setting for your story, including the geography, culture, and history of the world.

By practicing different writing exercises, you can refine your skills and gain a better understanding of what you excel at and what you need to work on.

6. Use Writing Tools.

In the process of finding your voice, writing tools can prove to be invaluable. These tools can help you identify your strengths and weaknesses, giving you feedback that can help you improve your craft. The tools range from physical books to digital programs, each with their unique advantages and applicabilities. Let's explore some of these tools and how they can benefit you as a writer.

Writing Tools That You Can Use Without An Outside Assistant

i. **Grammar books:** Books such as *The Elements of Style* by Strunk and White or *Eats, Shoots, & Leaves* by Lynne Truss can help you understand the fundamentals and nuances of English grammar. These books are compact, easy to reference, and can be read at your own pace. They offer clear examples of grammar rules, helping you to write more clearly and effectively.

ii. **Writing craft books:** Books like *On Writing* by Stephen King or *Bird by Bird* by Anne Lamott provide insights into the writing process from accomplished authors. They offer advice on character development, plot structure, and other key elements of storytelling. These books can serve as mentors in your writing journey.

iii. **Dictionaries and Thesauri:** A good dictionary and thesaurus are essential tools for any writer. They can help you find the right word and improve your vocabulary, allowing you to express your ideas more effectively. Personally, dictionary-wise, I like to use the 4th Edition college dictionaries. They're navy blue. The only thing worse than not knowing a word is finding that your dictionary doesn't know it either. I can't recall a time that these dictionaries didn't have a word I was looking for. Can't say the same for *Webster*.

iv. **Notebooks and Pens:** Being incarcerated authors, I know a lot of us have written on the back of Disciplinary Reports, Counselor Request, Store Sheet, or whatever other form of paper we could get our hands on at the time. However, the most basic tools of a writer are a notebook and a pen. These allow you to jot down ideas, draft stories, and revise your work. Regular writing practice is one of the best ways to improve your skills.

v. **Writing exercises and prompts:** Books like *The Writer's Idea Book* by Jack Heffron provide hundreds of writing prompts and exercises. These can help stimulate your creativity and develop your writing skills.

Writing Tools That Can Be Used With An Outside Assistant

i. **Grammarly:** This is an online tool that checks your grammar, spelling, punctuation, and style. It provides detailed explanations for its suggestions, helping you to understand and correct your mistakes. It requires internet access, so you can have an outside assistant input your text and provide you with the feedback.

ii. **Hemingway Editor:** This is another online tool that analyzes your writing to make it clear and powerful. It highlights complex sentences, adverb usage, and passive voice, among other things. Like Grammarly, it requires internet access so you would need an outside assistant to use it on your behalf.

iii. **Scrivener:** This is a software program that helps manage complex writing projects. It allows you to organize your thoughts, structure your manuscript, and keep track of your research. An outside assistant can use it to manage and structure your work as you dictate or send it.

iv. **ProWritingAid:** This online tool combines grammar checking with style suggestions to help improve the quality of your writing. It offers feedback on a range of writing issues like repetitiveness, vague wording, sentence length variation, and more. An outside assistant can use ProWritingAid to review your work and provide you with the feedback.

v. **Writing coaches or classes:** An outside assistant could hire a writing coach or enroll you in a writing class. This can provide personalized feedback and guidance to help you improve your writing. Some classes/coaches may correspond via traditional mail, providing another way to engage and learn from the outside world. Stratford Career Institute offers an affordable Creative Writing correspondence course, and it is one that I took myself. As of right now, 2023, the course total is $499 but you can get started for as little as $20 down and make payments of $31.93 a month. Here are a list of things that they cover below:

Writing Great Short Stories

- *Writing a short story—getting started*
- *Characters—How to create people who live and breathe on the page*
- *Conflict—How to devise a story that readers won't want to put down*
- *Plot and Structure—How to shape your story and keep it moving forward*
- *Setting and Atmosphere—How to bring readers into a vivid story world*

- *Narrative Voice—How to develop your individual voice as a writer*
- *Exploring the realm of short stories*
- *A quick guide to submitting manuscripts for publication*

Characters and Point of View

- *Two-dimensional words and three-dimensional characters*
- *Choosing point-of-view*
- *Story presentation*
- *Developing memorable characters*
- *Distinguishing main from minor characters*
- *Choosing the most effective viewpoint*

Description

- *Defining Description*
- *Genre Considerations*
- *How Point of View Brings Description to Life*
- *Making Description Serve the Story*
- *Recognizing Problematic Description*
- *Characteristics of Good Description*
- *Using the Five Senses in Fiction*
- *Metaphor and Simile*
- *Describing Setting, Characters, and Action*

．　．　．

Scene and Structure
- *Scenes as revelation of plot*
- *The steps leading towards climax and conclusion*
- *Developing scenes to build a story's structure*
- *Properly using cause and effect*
- *Unfolding the main character's struggle*
- *Building a believable and revealing end*

Write and Revise for Publication
- *Drafting, revising and fine-tuning your story*
- *Marketing your work*

On top of the skills that the course will give you and enhance, upon graduating, you will receive a copy of *Writer's Market* at no additional cost to you. I refer all my authors to this course, and now I'm referring you. If you're serious about writing, invest in yourself and take your pen to the next level.

vi. **Critique Partners and Writing Groups:** An outside assistant can help you connect with other writers for critique and feedback. They can transcribe your work and share it with the group, then relay their feedback to you. This can be a valuable way to get diverse perspectives on your writing from people who have no incentive to please you versus listening to the guys in your dorm cap you down about how good your writing is so they can ask you for a pack of noodles later on. Don't let them have you out here looking like Sam Sausage Head. Getting feedback from publishing professionals can be even more valuable. Consider hiring a professional editor or writing coach to review your work and provide feedback on your strengths and weaknesses as a writer. A professional editor or writing coach can offer objective feedback on your writing, as well as provide guidance on how to improve your craft. They can also help you identify your unique voice as a writer and develop a writing style that resonates with readers.

vii. **Voice to Text Software:** If you have the ability to make phone calls to your outside assistant, you can use voice-to-text software. You dictate your story over the phone, and the software transcribes your words into text. This can be a powerful way to generate text if you enjoy speaking more than writing, or if it helps you to think more freely. In my opinion, though, this will be a headache out this world. Voice to Text software a lot of times hardly picks up correctly when you do it yourself over the phone. Saying, "Tyra got up and went to the refrigerator." may come out like, "Tired of got up and went to the refrigerator." That's a lot of errors in your document for no reason when you could simply write it out. Same time, some people would rather get the bulk of it down this way then go back through and make the corrections. Everyone has their preferences. So, while this is not one of mine, I still felt I should list it as an option.

viii. **Traditional Publishing Houses and Literary Agents:** When you feel your manuscript is ready, an outside assistant can help you submit your work to traditional publishing houses or literary agents. They can research submission guidelines, prepare your manuscript, write query letters, and send them on your behalf. I went through a period in the beginning of my writing career where I was looking into how much it would cost to have a literary agent find me a publisher. I found out that you don't pay them. They get a percentage of whatever deal they get you, which is usually 15 to 20%. The frustrating thing is that you submit your manuscript to them very much the same way you would submit it to a publisher, and more times than not, you won't get a response. But...Peter Paul said, "try 'em all."

Remember, all these tools are just that – tools. They can guide you and help you hone your craft, but they can't replace the creativity, passion, and unique voice that you bring to your writing. Keep writing, keep learning, and never lose sight of your unique voice and vision.

7. Embrace Your Unique Voice.

Again, it's important to embrace your unique voice as a writer. Your voice is what sets you apart from other writers, and it's what makes your work authentic and engaging. Don't be afraid to experiment with different writing styles and techniques, but also don't try to force yourself to write in a way that doesn't feel natural. Embrace your strengths and weaknesses and use them to develop a voice that is unique to you.

8. Consider Your Audience.

When identifying your writing strengths and weaknesses, it's important to consider your target audience. Urban fiction readers have specific expectations when it comes to the style and content of the books they read. Understanding these expectations can help you tailor your writing to meet their needs.

For example, urban fiction readers often expect fast-paced, action-packed stories with relatable characters and authentic dialogue. They also tend to appreciate stories that explore social issues and themes relevant to their own experiences.

By considering your target audience when identifying your writing strengths and weaknesses, you can gain a better understanding of what works and what doesn't in urban fiction.

9. Keep Learning and Growing

Identifying your writing strengths and weaknesses is not a one-time event. As you continue to write and publish, you will likely discover new strengths and weaknesses that you were not aware of before. It's important to approach your writing with a *growth* mindset, always looking for opportunities to learn and improve.

By staying open to feedback and committing to ongoing growth, you can continue to refine your writing and develop a unique voice that resonates with readers.

In conclusion, identifying your writing strengths and weaknesses is a crucial step towards developing your voice as an urban fiction writer. By reflecting on your past experiences, analyzing your writing style, reading widely, seeking feedback from others, practicing writing exercises, using writing tools, and embracing your unique voice, you can create compelling and authentic stories that resonate with your readers.

Identifying your writing strengths and weaknesses is an ongoing process that requires self-reflection, feedback from others, and a commitment to growth. By considering your target audience, seeking professional feedback, and staying open to learning and growth, you can develop a writing voice that is authentic, engaging, and uniquely your own.

Reading and Learning from Other Authors

Reading and learning from other authors is a powerful way to develop your voice as a writer. This not only helps you develop your own unique voice, but also exposes you to different styles, techniques, and perspectives. In this section, we will delve into how to read and learn from other authors, including tips for selecting books to read, analyzing writing styles, and applying lessons learned to your own writing.

Selecting Books to Read

1. **Choose books within your genre:** As an Urban Fiction writer, you will benefit the most by reading books within the genre. This will help you understand the conventions, themes, and techniques that are specific to Urban Fiction. Look for titles by popular authors like Teri Woods, K'wan, and Sister Souljah. Additionally, don't limit yourself to just recent releases; explore classic Urban Fiction books as well.

2. **Read books from diverse authors:** To broaden your understanding and perspective, read works by authors from different backgrounds, genders, and ethnicities. This will expose you to a variety of voices, stories, and experiences that can inspire and inform your own writing. Some of my personal favorites are John Grisham, James Patterson, Dean Koontz, David Baldacci, and Stuart Woods.

.   .   .

3. **Explore other genres:** While it's important to read within your genre, don't be afraid to venture into other genres as well. Reading books from different genres, such as mystery, romance, or science fiction, can help you understand how other authors approach storytelling and character development. This can provide valuable insights that you can apply to your Urban Fiction writing.

Analyzing Writing Styles

1. **Pay attention to the author's voice:** As you read, take note of the author's distinct voice and style. Consider how their word choice, sentence structure, and tone contribute to the overall feel of the story. Ask yourself what makes their voice unique and how you can incorporate similar techniques into your own writing.

2. **Analyze character development:** Characters are at the heart of any Urban Fiction story, so it's crucial to study how other authors create compelling, relatable, and dynamic characters. Pay attention to how characters are introduced, how their backstory is revealed, and how their relationships with other characters evolve throughout the story.

3. **Study dialogue:** Dialogue is a powerful tool that can reveal character, advance the plot, and create tension. Notice how other authors use dialogue to convey information, develop character relationships, and maintain the pace of the story. Analyze the balance between dialogue and narration

and think about how you can use dialogue effectively in your own writing.

4. Examine plot structure: Urban Fiction often involves intricate plots with multiple storylines and twists. As you read, break down the plot structure and consider how the author builds tension, foreshadows events, and resolves conflicts. This will help you understand how to create engaging and suspenseful stories that keep readers hooked.

Applying Lessons Learned to Your Own Writing

1. **Experiment with different techniques:** After analyzing other authors' writing styles and techniques, try incorporating some of their methods into your own writing. This might include adopting a particular tone, experimenting with sentence structure, or writing from different perspectives. Remember, the goal is not to imitate another author's style, but to learn from it and develop your own unique voice.

2. **Practice, practice, practice:** Becoming a skilled writer takes time and consistent effort. The more you write, the more you will learn about yourself as a writer and develop your unique voice. Set aside time each day or week to write, even if it's just for a few minutes. As you practice, apply the lessons you've learned from reading other authors and analyzing their techniques.

3. **Revise and edit your work:** I know you may be tired of

seeing this one, and a few others I may have mentioned more than once in a different way, but like those things, writing is a process, and revision is a crucial part of that process. After completing a draft, take some time to step away from it, and then return to it with fresh eyes. As you revise, consider how you can improve your voice, characters, dialogue, and plot structure based on what you've learned from other authors. Don't be afraid to make significant changes if it will strengthen your story.

4. **Find a writing partner:** Connecting with other writers can be incredibly beneficial, especially if you're in a challenging environment like prison. The support and feedback from fellow writers can help you grow and refine your craft. If forming a writing group isn't possible, consider finding a writing partner with whom you can exchange work and provide constructive feedback.

5. **Stay open to learning:** As a writer, you should always be open to learning and growing. Continue reading and analyzing the work of other authors and be receptive to feedback and new ideas. The more you learn, the more your writing will improve and evolve.

6. **Take notes while reading:** As you read books by other authors, keep a notebook or journal handy to jot down any striking passages, descriptions, or techniques that you find particularly effective or inspiring. Later, you can review these notes and consider how to incorporate similar elements or approaches into your own writing.

7. **Study the pacing of stories:** The pace at which a story unfolds can greatly impact its overall effectiveness. As you read, observe how authors control the pace of their narratives, balancing action, dialogue, and description. Analyze how they create a sense of urgency or slow down the story to build tension or suspense. This understanding can help you determine the best pacing for your own stories.

8. **Examine world-building:** Urban Fiction often involves creating vivid, immersive settings that feel authentic to readers. Pay attention to how authors develop their story's world, using details, imagery, and cultural references to bring it to life. Consider how you can create a similarly rich and engaging world for your characters and readers to inhabit.

9. **Learn from authors' successes and failures:** Not every book you read will be a masterpiece, and that's okay. As a writer, you can learn as much from a poorly executed story as you can from a well-crafted one. Analyze both successful and less successful works to understand what does and doesn't work in terms of voice, character development, plot structure, and more.

10. **Develop a writing routine:** Establishing a consistent writing routine can help you make steady progress on your work, even in a challenging environment like prison. Find a time and place that works best for you and commit to writing regularly. This will help you develop your skills and maintain momentum on your projects.

· · ·

By incorporating these additional tips and strategies into your approach to reading and learning from other authors, you'll be better equipped to develop your unique voice and strengthen your writing. Remember that growth and improvement as a writer is an ongoing process, so stay committed to learning and evolving throughout your journey.

Simply put, reading and learning from other authors is a powerful way to develop your voice as a writer, particularly in Urban Fiction. By selecting the right books to read, analyzing writing styles, and applying lessons learned to your own writing, you can become a more skilled and confident writer. Remember that finding your voice and honing your craft is a journey, so be patient and persistent in your efforts. As you continue to learn from the works of others, you'll be well on your way to publishing a compelling and successful book from prison.

Overcoming Writer's Block and Creative Resistance

Writer's block and creative resistance can stem from various sources. Understanding these causes can help you devise a more effective approach to overcoming these obstacles. Here are a few common reasons why people experience writer's block:

1.**Fear of Judgement:** Many writers fear criticism or rejection, which can cause them to second-guess their work and ultimately, hinder their writing process.

2. **Perfectionism:** Striving for perfection can lead to writer's block. When a writer is overly concerned about every sentence being perfect, they may find it difficult to progress.

3. **Lack of Motivation:** Sometimes, writers may lack the motivation to write due to a lack of interest, fatigue, or other personal issues. This is why it's so important to write the stories you're passionate about. People who write for the sake of *passion* versus the sake of money, often last longer and have the most successful writing careers. When you experience writer's block for this reason, it's time to go back to the drawing board and fall in love with the characters again. Ask yourself...what was so special about them that you felt their story needed to be told in the first place?

4. **Overwhelm:** The enormity of a project can often cause writer's block. The writer may feel overwhelmed by the amount of work that needs to be done or by the complexity of the subject matter.

5. **Emotional Distress:** Stress, depression, anxiety, and other emotional states can significantly impact a person's ability to write.

6. **Physical Environment:** In some cases, the physical environment may not be conducive to writing. This can be particularly relevant for individuals writing from prison, where the environment may be noisy, chaotic, or lacking privacy. Personally, I've got so used to the noise, I can write through it. The chaos motivates me and can even be content

for scenes (read my book *Murda Was The Case 2: Never Forget Loyalty*). As far as privacy, I've written in a cell, on the yard, at the table in the dorm. Doesn't matter. It's all a mind thing at the end of the day.

Now that we understand the causes of writer's block, here are some practical tips to overcome it:

1. **Break Down Your Task:** Large tasks can seem daunting. Break down your writing project into smaller, manageable tasks. Instead of trying to write an entire chapter, focus on a single paragraph or even a sentence.

2. **Set a Routine:** Having a regular writing schedule can significantly reduce writer's block. Try to find a specific time each day to write, even if you're not feeling particularly inspired.

3. **Change Your Environment:** If possible, change your physical environment. This could mean moving to a different location within your cell or making your existing space more conducive to writing.

4. **Free writing:** This technique involves writing continuously for a set amount of time without worrying about grammar, punctuation, or topic. The goal is to let your thoughts flow freely and get your creative juices flowing.

5. **Mind Mapping:** This tool can help you visualize your ideas and how they relate to each other, which can spark creativity and help overcome writer's block.

6. **Physical Activity:** Physical activity can stimulate creativity. If possible, take a short walk, do some stretching, or engage in any other form of exercise available to you.

7. **Seek Feedback:** Sharing your work with others can provide you with a fresh perspective and constructive criticism that can help improve your writing and motivate you to move forward.

8. **Practice Mindfulness:** Mindfulness and meditation can reduce stress and anxiety, increase focus, and boost creativity. Even a few minutes of mindfulness each day can be beneficial.

9. **Accept Imperfection:** No piece of writing is perfect in its first draft. Accepting this fact can alleviate the pressure and help you move forward.

10. **Affirmations:** Positive self-talk can boost your confidence and reduce the fear of criticism or rejection.

11. **Read Widely:** Reading can inspire ideas and stimulate your imagination. It can expose you to different styles and approaches to writing. Try to read a variety of materials, including books, magazines, and newspapers, if they are accessible to you.

12. **Journaling:** Keeping a daily journal can help you develop discipline and consistency in your writing. It can also serve as a repository for ideas, thoughts, and reflections that you can refer back to.

13. **Limit Distractions:** Distractions can break your focus and make it difficult to write. While it may be challenging in

a prison environment, try to create a quiet, distraction-free space for your writing time.

14. **Use Prompts:** Writing prompts can help you get started when you're feeling stuck. They can be a single word, a sentence, or a scenario that can spur your imagination and get you writing.

15. **Explore Different Genres:** If you're stuck in your usual writing style or genre, try exploring different ones. Writing a poem, a short story, or even a letter can help you break out of a rut.

16. **Write for Yourself First:** Write the story you want to tell, not the one you think others want to read. This can free you from the constraints of pleasing others and allow your creativity to flow more freely.

17. **Use Imagery:** Visualize scenes in your mind before you write them. This can help you describe settings, characters, and actions more vividly and make your story more engaging.

18. **Practice Patience:** Overcoming writer's block takes time. Don't rush the process. Allow yourself to rest when needed, and remember that progress, no matter how slow, is still progress.

19. **Remember Your 'Why':** Remind yourself why you want to write. Whether it's to tell your story, to express your thoughts and feelings, or to seek a sense of fulfillment, keeping your 'why' in mind can inspire and motivate you to keep going.

. . .

Overcoming writer's block and creative resistance is a journey, not a destination. It involves exploring, experimenting, and learning about yourself as a writer. By applying these strategies and maintaining a positive and patient mindset, you can continue to grow and evolve as a writer, regardless of your circumstances.

Remember, every writer experiences periods of creative resistance. The key is to not let these periods discourage you. Instead, see them as opportunities to explore new strategies, techniques, and ideas. With patience, perseverance, and practice, you can overcome writer's block and continue your creative journey, even from within the confines of a prison cell.

Finding Support and Community

Writing can be a solitary pursuit, but it's important to find **support and community** as you develop your voice as an author. I spoke about this briefly earlier on in this book but I wanted to expound on it a little more.

As an urban fiction author publishing from prison, finding support and community can be difficult. However, it is crucial to have a network of individuals who can offer guidance, feedback, and encouragement throughout the writing and publishing process.

One way to find support and community is through writing groups or workshops. Many correctional facilities offer writing programs and book clubs, which provide opportunities to connect with other writers and receive feedback on your work. Additionally, there are several organizations that provide writing resources and support to incarcerated individuals, one of which is the PEN America's Prison Writing Program.

PEN America's Prison Writing Program's book, *The Handbook For Writers In Prison,* was the first book I had about writing when I decided I was going to give the literary world a real shot. It's basic but if nothing else, it helped me understand the difference between first, second, and third person POV's, and it gave me some insight on grammar and punctuation. You can send them a letter requesting a copy and they'll send you one for free. Here is their address:

PEN America Center
588 Broadway #303
New York, NY 10012

Another way to connect with other writers and readers is through social media. Platforms like Twitter and Instagram can be powerful tools for building a following and connecting with other writers in the urban fiction genre. Joining online writing communities or participating in writing challenges can also provide opportunities to connect with other writers and receive feedback on your work.

It is also important to seek out mentors who can offer guidance and support throughout the writing and publishing process. This can be challenging from within a correctional facility, but there are organizations that offer mentorship programs specifically for incarcerated writers, such as the nonprofit organization, Free Minds Book Club & Writing Workshop.

Finally, it is important to remember that writing can be somewhat draining at times, and it is important to prioritize self-care and mental health. Taking time for yourself, whether it be through meditation, exercise, or simply finding a quiet space to reflect, can help you stay grounded and focused on your writing goals, especially if you have a lot going on.

Conclusion

In conclusion, finding support and community as an author publishing from prison can be challenging, but it is crucial to have a network of individuals who can offer guidance, feedback, and encouragement throughout the writing and publishing process. By taking advantage of writing programs, social media, mentorship opportunities, and prioritizing self-care, you can build a strong support system and develop your voice as an author.

Developing Your Story

"I do my due diligence to be the best."
— *JaQuavis Coleman*

Welcome to one of the most exciting aspects of your book-writing journey – *Developing Your Story.* This is where you transform your concepts, experiences, and insights into a compelling narrative that engages, informs, and moves your readers. Your story is the heart and soul of your book; it's what makes your work stand out from the crowd and resonates with your readers on a profound level.

Writing from an unconventional location like prison adds an extra layer of depth and intrigue to your story. It propels your narrative beyond the ordinary, offering a unique perspective that can powerfully impact your readers. It's more than just about making your book interesting; it's about making it *unforgettable*.

In this chapter, we're going to delve into the art and science of story development. I'll explore the different types of stories you can tell – from personal narratives and memoirs to thought-provoking insights. I'll help you discover your unique story type and guide you on how to use it most effectively.

We'll also discuss how to structure your book for maximum impact. A well-structured book isn't just easy to follow; it's engaging, persuasive, and satisfying. I'll introduce you to different structuring techniques, giving you the tools to create a narrative arc that keeps your readers hooked from the first page to the last.

Additionally, we'll address the unique challenges and opportunities that come with writing a book from prison. I'll provide tips and strategies to effectively harness your unique circumstances and transform them into compelling story-telling.

Whether you're writing fiction, sharing your personal journey, offering a unique perspective, or teaching valuable lessons, this chapter will guide you in creating a powerful narrative that captures your readers' attention and leaves a lasting impression.

. . .

Let's get it!

Finding Your Story

The first step in developing your story is *finding the story you want to tell*. This can be a challenging process, but it's important to tap into your experiences, emotions, and perspectives to find a story that is uniquely yours. In prison, you may have limited resources and opportunities, but you can still find inspiration in your surroundings and experiences. Take the time to reflect on your life and find the story that you want to share with the world or go listen to the guy in the dorm who's always telling them lies about what he had, where he been, and what he did on the street. Y'all know who I'm talking about. Yea, him right there. Probably lying now.

Anyways, my point is that there are stories everywhere, especially in prison. One of my partnas played a joke on me before. We were in the hole and decided to exchange Street Lit novels. I sent him, *Hittaz: Get It Back In Blood* by Lou Garden Price, Sr. Moments later, the orderly brought me back my partnas' paperwork. Yes, his court discovery packet. Till this day we laugh about it, but I realize a true fact: every discovery packet is a Urban Fiction novel.

Am I telling you to go around reading everyone's discovery packet? No. That'll probably get you wet up. What I am saying is much like every inmate has a discovery packet, every inmate has a story — a few of 'em. Back in 2016, when I was still trying to figure all this publishing stuff out, I had come across a blog post written by a federal inmate named Christopher Zoukis, a popular *Prison Legal News* contributor. In it, he mentioned that submitting short stories in contests and anthologies was a good way incarcerated aspiring authors could gain traction and get their names out there. That in mind, it was placed on my to-do list as a task but I had no plot in mind for a short story.

Not long after that, I found myself in the hole once again, and this time with a cool guy maybe five or so years older than me from Atlanta. He liked to smoke gas, and when he got high, he talked my head off about the city for hours. I would be kicked back, listening, because they were actually interesting and felt real. He wasn't capped up like a lot of people be. In his stories he had it at times, and sometimes he was down bad. It got funny at times, and sometimes it was sad. Then one day I asked him if he believed in roots. He said, "he did" and explained why.

The story to his explanation got my gears turning. I didn't want to write a paranormal urban tale, but it was a dope idea I had. I got him some gas from the orderly the next morning and had him run the story back by me along with a few other stories he had told me, this time taking notes. A few days later I had written my first short story, *"Money Blessings."*

I never was able to get it in a contest or anthology, so I put it in my own short story collection titled, *Tales 4rm Da Dale: A*

Short Story Collection. It's the first story in the book and is still one of my favorite stories I've penned till this day, hands down.

Let people, events, and your imagination tell the stories, you just write them. Keep a writer's journal handy, too. Not a journal, like a diary, but a journal that you write ideas, quotes, and other things down that you may add to a story in the future. There's always a story to be told. You just have to find it.

Understanding Your Audience

When writing fiction, one of the most important aspects you should consider is *your audience.* Who are they? What do they like? What kind of stories do they want to read? By answering these questions, you can tailor your narrative to meet the needs and expectations of your readers, which will increase the likelihood of your book being read and enjoyed.

I. General Fiction Audience.

In general, fiction readers appreciate compelling characters, engaging plots, and immersive world-building. They want to be transported into a different world, where they can experience new and exciting adventures through the eyes of your characters. To appeal to this audience, focus on creating realistic characters with depth and complexity, plot twists that keep readers on their toes, and detailed settings that draw readers into your story.

2. Genre-Specific Audiences.

Different genres attract different types of readers, each with their own set of preferences. For instance, mystery readers enjoy puzzles and suspense, while romance readers prefer emotional depth and relationship development. Science fiction and fantasy readers value imaginative world-building and thought-provoking themes, while historical fiction readers appreciate meticulous research and accuracy. Understand the conventions of your chosen genre and use them to shape your story.

3. Urban Fiction Audience.

Urban Fiction, also known as Street Lit, often portrays the gritty realities of city life, with themes revolving around survival, resilience, and the pursuit of better circumstances. It typically features characters who are grappling with societal issues such as poverty, crime, and racial inequality. This genre's audience often seeks authentic, raw narratives that reflect their own experiences or illuminate the lives of others in similar situations. **Translation: HOOD SHIT!**

To write effective Urban Fiction, it's crucial to create a genuine portrayal of the streets. *"If you real, they gonna come see about you,"* JaQuavis Coleman says. A lot of authors now days aren't qualified to write for this genre and it shows. They're giving the game a black eye. If you ain't street, park yo pen. Urban Fiction readers appreciate realistic dialogue, nuanced characters who are products of their environment, and plotlines that reflect the challenges and triumphs of city living. Our lived experiences can offer invaluable insights. That said, remember the importance of research. Even if you're writing about a place or culture you're familiar with, verifying your facts and understanding the broader context is crucial in building a believable world. Remember, authenticity is key. Your readers will know if you've done your research and if your portrayal of the streets ring true.

4. Audience Demographics.

Also consider the demographics of your potential readers. Are they young adults, adults, or seniors? Are they predominantly male, female, or a mix of genders? What are their cultural backgrounds? What are their interests and values? This information can help you create characters and plotlines that your readers can identify with and care about. It will also be helpful to know when it comes time for marketing. For example, Facebook Ad categories are location, interests, gender, and age. Knowing your audience demographics can allow you to target them more affectively. We'll talk more about this in Chapter 8.

. . .

5. Reader Expectations.

Finally, consider your readers' expectations. What do they hope to gain by reading your book? Are they looking for an escape, a thrilling adventure, a deep emotional experience, or a new perspective on life? By understanding and meeting these expectations, you can create a story that not only entertains but also resonates with your readers.

Remember, writing is a form of communication, and *effective communication* requires an understanding of the receiver. By understanding your audience, you can craft a story that speaks to them on a deep, personal level. This, in turn, will increase the likelihood of your book being read, enjoyed, and recommended to others.

Understanding your audience is a vital part of developing your story, a step you cannot afford to miss. Your story will not exist in a vacuum; it will be read and interpreted by people. To ensure that your message gets across and that your story impacts your readers in the way you want it to, you must know who your readers are and what they want.

Crafting Your Narrative

Crafting a narrative is an empowering process. It's about taking control of your own story, shaping it, and sharing it with others. For an incarcerated individual, this can be a profound journey of self-discovery and personal expression. Through it, you can explore the breadth and depth of human experience, your own included, and create something meaningful that resonates with readers. This section introduces the basics of narrative crafting, with a special emphasis on Urban Fiction.

<u>Fundamentals of Fiction</u>

Regardless of genre, all fiction shares some *foundational elements*: characters, plot, setting, theme, and style.

Characters are the heart and soul of your story; they are the vehicles through which your readers experience the narrative. Make them as real as possible, with their own hopes, fears, strengths, and flaws.

The *plot* is the sequence of events that make up your story. A good plot is more than just a random series of events—it should follow a structure that includes a beginning, middle, and end, with a compelling conflict and resolution.

The *setting* is where and when your story takes place. It can be as specific as a prison cell or as broad as a sprawling urban landscape. The setting is more than just a backdrop for action; it can influence characters' behaviors and decisions, shape the plot, and lend depth to the narrative.

The *theme* is the underlying message or central idea of your story. Themes can be complex and multi-faceted, and they often touch on universal human experiences and emotions.

Style refers to the way you tell your story. It includes your choice of words, sentence structure, and tone. Your style can drastically affect how your story is received.

Urban Fiction

Urban Fiction, also known as Street Lit or Hip-Hop Fiction, is a genre that thrives on authenticity. It often draws inspiration from the struggles and triumphs of individuals living in city environments, particularly those from marginalized communities. This genre is rich with raw emotion, complex relationships, and social commentary. While the settings are often gritty and realistic, the characters' resilience, creativity, and determination shine through.

Furthermore, Urban Fiction often involves characters who are coping with challenging situations. It's important to portray these characters with empathy and respect. Even if they make choices that the reader might not agree with, the goal is to present them as real people with their own motivations and circumstances; or simply put, just like me and you.

Conclusion

Crafting your narrative is a deeply personal process. It's about finding your voice and using it to tell stories that resonate with you and your readers. Whether you're writing a sprawling fantasy epic, a hard-boiled detective story, or a gritty urban drama, the goal is the same: to create a compelling, character-driven story that offers insight into the human experience. So, *take the reins of your narrative.* Explore, experiment, and most importantly, express yourself. Your unique perspective is your greatest asset as a writer.

Adding Depth and Dimension to Your Characters

1. Creating Backstories

Your character's past can significantly shape their present actions, attitudes, and decisions. When developing your character's backstory, consider key life events, their upbringing, and past relationships. These elements can help explain your character's motivations, fears, and desires. For example, a character who grew up in a strict environment might value freedom and rebel against authority. Remember, however, that a backstory should not be a laundry list of past events; it should provide insights into why a character is the way they are.

2. Developing Personalities

Character personalities are essential for making your

characters feel like *real people*. Consider different personality traits, like extraversion or introversion, agreeableness, conscientiousness, emotional stability, and openness to experiences. A character's personality should be consistent but not one-dimensional. Real people have a mix of traits, and they may behave differently in different situations or change over time. Also, consider how your character's personality traits may conflict with their goals or desires. This can create interesting internal conflict and character development.

3. Writing Believable Dialogue

Dialogue is a great tool for revealing character. Through dialogue, you can show a character's personality, attitudes, and even their past without explicitly stating it. To write believable dialogue, consider your character's background, education, and personality. A character's speech should reflect these aspects. For example, an educated character might use complex sentences and a broad vocabulary, while a more straightforward character might speak in simple, direct sentences. Also, pay attention to the rhythm and flow of dialogue. Real people often speak in fragments and interrupt each other, and they use body language and tone of voice to convey meaning.

In my story, *"Wet Dreams On Lockdown: The Nurse,"* these elements took on even more depth, and rightly so. In a prison setting, your characters might be prisoners, guards, family members, or lawyers, each with unique backstories and perspectives. The prison environment can shape their personalities and create complex, high-stakes conflicts. Their dialogue can reveal the harsh realities of life behind the wall and their efforts to maintain dignity and hope in a challenging environment.

4. Incorporating Authentic Experiences

In a setting as unique and charged as a prison, it's important to incorporate authentic experiences. Someone who's never been to prison writing about it might research the living conditions, daily routines, and rules in prison. This could help them create characters that feel real and grounded in their environment. Furthermore, consider the emotional and psychological impact of prison life on your characters. This can add another layer of depth and complexity to them.

5. Balancing Strengths and Flaws

Every person has strengths and flaws, and so should your characters. I'm going to use prison again because I know if you're reading this, it's something you can relate to. Balancing strengths and flaws is especially important in a prison setting, where *flaws* can lead to dramatic consequences and *strengths* can be a lifeline. Perhaps a character's strength is their intelligence, which helps them navigate the complex prison social hierarchy, but their flaw is their short temper, which gets them into trouble. Balancing strengths and flaws can make your characters more relatable and engaging.

Remember, your characters are the heart of your story. By adding depth and dimension to them, you can create characters that are not only interesting to read about, but also *feel* real and compelling. They will carry your reader through the ups and downs of your narrative, making the journey more immersive and emotionally impactful.

6. Creating a Sense of Place and Atmosphere

Creating a sense of place and atmosphere is a crucial aspect of storytelling across all genres of fiction. Whether you're developing a gritty urban narrative, a fantasy epic, or a suspenseful thriller, the setting should be more than just a backdrop for your characters' actions. It should be a living, breathing entity that shapes their experiences and influences their decisions. In this section, we'll explore how to create vivid, immersive environments that will transport your readers into your story world.

7. The Importance of Sensory Details

One of the most effective ways to create a sense of place

and atmosphere is through the use of sensory details. These are descriptions that engage the reader's five senses: *sight, sound, touch, taste, and smell*. When used effectively, sensory details can make your readers feel as if they are experiencing the story firsthand.

For example, in urban fiction, you might describe the clamor of a bustling city street, the smell of exhaust fumes mixed with street food, or the feel of gritty pavement under a character's feet. The key is to be *specific and evocative*. Instead of simply stating that a neighborhood is run-down, describe the peeling paint on the buildings, the cracked sidewalks, or the rusty, squeaking swings in the park. This level of detail can make your setting feel real and tangible.

8. Setting Descriptions: More Than Just Locations

While physical descriptions are important, creating a sense of place and atmosphere goes beyond just describing the physical environment. It's also about conveying the mood, culture, and spirit of a place. This can be achieved through the use of imagery and symbolism, as well as through the interactions and experiences of your characters.

In urban fiction, the city itself often becomes a character. It's not just a location; it's a living, breathing entity that influences the characters and the story. The city might be portrayed as a place of opportunity or a place of hardship. It could be a source of community and belonging, or it could be a source of conflict and struggle.

To create this kind of depth, think about the symbolic aspects of your setting. What does the city represent to your characters? How does it influence their actions and decisions? How does it shape their perceptions and experiences? By exploring these questions, you can create a setting that is rich and layered, one that adds depth and complexity to your narrative.

9. Imagery: Painting a Picture with Words

Imagery is another powerful tool for creating a sense of place and atmosphere. By using evocative language and vivid descriptions, you can paint a mental picture that immerses your readers in your story world.

For example, in a suspenseful thriller set in a remote, isolated location, you might use imagery to create a sense of unease or foreboding. You could describe the eerie silence of the woods; the stark, unending expanses of empty land; or the shadows that seem to lurk in every corner.

In urban fiction, imagery can be used to highlight the stark contrasts of city life. You could describe the glaring neon lights of a busy street; the stark, imposing facades of high-rise buildings; or the vibrant, chaotic energy of a crowded market. The key is to use language that is vivid and evocative, that paints a picture in the reader's mind and makes them feel as if they are there, experiencing the scene firsthand.

10. Capturing the Rhythm of Life

Creating an authentic sense of place also requires capturing the rhythm of life in your chosen setting. This means paying attention to the patterns of daily life, the local customs and traditions, the language and dialects used by the locals, and the social dynamics within the community.

In urban fiction, this might involve describing the hustle and bustle of the morning commute, the vibrant street life, the interactions between different groups and communities, or the impact of social issues like poverty, crime, or gentrification. It's these details that can make your setting feel alive and dynamic.

11. Reflecting Inner Landscapes

Remember, the outer world often reflects the inner world of your characters. The atmosphere and mood of your setting can be used to mirror or contrast with your character's emotional state. For example, a desolate, abandoned cityscape could reflect a character's feelings of loneliness and isolation. A bustling, crowded market could serve as a metaphor for a character's inner turmoil or confusion.

In urban fiction, the city itself can be a powerful symbol

for the character's inner landscapes. The towering skyscrapers could symbolize their ambitions or aspirations. The rough, gritty streets could reflect their struggles or hardships. The vibrant, pulsating energy of the city could mirror their hopes, dreams, or desires.

12. Practice Makes Perfect

Creating a sense of place and atmosphere is a skill that requires practice. Start by observing your own environment closely. Pay attention to the sensory details, the rhythm of daily life, and the ways in which the physical environment reflects the inner lives of the people who live there. Then, try to incorporate these observations into your writing.

Remember, your goal is not to create a detailed travelogue or a dry, factual description. Your goal is to create an immersive, evocative environment that draws your readers in and makes them feel as if they are part of your story world.

Conclusion

Mastering the art of creating a sense of place and atmosphere can elevate your writing and make your stories more engaging and compelling. Whether you're writing urban fiction or any other genre, remember that your setting is more than just a backdrop for your character's actions. It's a living, breathing entity that shapes their experiences and influences their decisions. So, take the time to create a setting that is vivid, immersive, and rich in sensory detail. Your readers will thank you for it.

Adding Conflict and Tension

Conflict and tension are central to storytelling because they create a dynamic narrative that engages the reader or audience, propelling the story forward and providing a framework for character development and thematic exploration. Here's a detailed examination of why these elements are so crucial:

1. **Driving the Plot Forward:** Conflict is the engine of a story. It arises from the protagonist's desire to achieve a goal and the obstacles that stand in their way. Without conflict, there is no plot, merely a series of events. *Tension* is the byproduct of this conflict—it keeps readers wondering what will happen next and how the characters will handle the challenges they face.

2. **Character Development:** Conflict forces characters to make choices and take action, revealing their values, motivations, and personalities. As characters respond to conflict, they are often forced to grow and change, a process that is at the heart of character arcs.

Tension adds depth to these arcs by creating uncertainty about the character's fates, making their development more compelling.

3. **Engagement and Emotion:** Conflict and tension engage readers emotionally. Readers become invested in the characters and their struggles, rooting for them to overcome their challenges. This emotional investment is what keeps readers turning the pages. Tension, in particular, evokes emotions such as worry, excitement, and anticipation, which can create a visceral reading experience.

4. **Creating Stakes:** Conflict establishes what is at stake in a story. It clarifies the consequences of failure and success for the protagonist. Tension heightens these stakes by prolonging the uncertainty around the outcome. The higher the stakes, the more gripping the story, as readers become anxious about the potential loss or hopeful for the character's success.

5. **Pacing and Dynamics:** Conflict and tension are key tools for controlling the pacing of a story. A writer can ramp up the tension to quicken the pace or introduce moments of lesser conflict to provide readers with a breather. This dynamic pacing helps to maintain interest and prevents the story from becoming monotonous.

6. **Thematic Exploration:** Conflict provides a narrative space to explore themes and ideas. It can be used to highlight struggles within society, human nature, or the human condition. Tension keeps these themes at the forefront of the reader's mind by continually reminding them of the ongoing struggle.

7. **Relatability and Catharsis:** Conflict is relatable because it mirrors the challenges of real life. Readers can sympathize with characters facing difficulties, which makes the story more compelling and immersive. Tension builds up emotional energy that can lead to catharsis—the release of strong emotions as the story reaches its climax and resolution.

8. **Surprise and Unpredictability:** Conflict often leads to unexpected developments that surprise the reader, while tension can make even predictable events feel suspenseful. This unpredictability keeps readers intrigued and can subvert clichés, making the story feel fresh and original.

9. **Moral and Ethical Complexity:** Conflicts often force characters to confront moral or ethical dilemmas, adding layers of complexity to the narrative. This can create tension not only within the plot but also within the characters themselves,

as they struggle with their decisions and the implications of their actions.

10. **Setting and World-Building:** Conflict can arise from the world itself, whether it's a hostile environment, a society with oppressive rules, or a supernatural threat. This allows for rich world-building and can create an omnipresent tension that shapes the characters and the story they inhabit.

Conclusion

In summary, conflict and tension are not just tools to make a story more exciting; they are fundamental to the narrative structure. They make stories meaningful and memorable by connecting with readers on an emotional level, challenging characters, and prompting readers to think about larger themes and questions. Without conflict and tension, stories would lack depth, purpose, and the power to resonate with their audience.

In conclusion, conflict and tension are the warp and weft that weave together the fabric of a story, giving it texture, color, and strength. They ensure that a narrative is not just a passive recounting of events, but a living, breathing process of transformation that mirrors the complexities of life itself. Stories thrive on these elements, as they form the core of a tale's ability to captivate, move, and ultimately, connect with its audience. Understanding the pivotal role of conflict and tension is essential for any storyteller aiming to craft a compelling narrative.

As we turn the page to the next section, "Creating Obstacles," we build upon this foundation of conflict and tension to explore how the deliberate placement of hurdles not only enhances the aforementioned elements but actively shapes the journey of our characters. Obstacles are the specific manifestations of conflict that require our protagonists to dig deep, struggle, adapt, and evolve. They are the tangible touchstones of tension that make the abstract concept of conflict intensely personal and immediate for both characters and readers. By creating obstacles that are meaningful and formidable, a storyteller challenges their characters to strive harder and grow, making their eventual triumphs—or failures—resonate all the more with the reader.

Creating Obstacles

Obstacles are often the most direct way to introduce conflict and tension into your story. They can come in many forms, from a physical barrier that a character must overcome, to a personal weakness or even a societal restriction. The key here is to make sure the obstacle is relevant to the story and the character's goals. An obstacle should challenge a character, but it should also allow for growth and development. It should force them to confront their flaws or fears, and ultimately come out stronger on the other side.

Developing Plot Twists

Plot twists can also add a significant amount of tension to your story. These unexpected turns or revelations can throw both your characters and your readers off balance, keeping them engaged and invested in the story. When developing a plot twist, it's important to find the right balance between surprise and believability. A twist should be unexpected, but it should also make sense in the context of the story. Foreshadowing can be a useful tool here, as it allows you to plant clues that make the twist feel earned, rather than arbitrary.

Building Suspense

Suspense is another tool that can be used to heighten tension and keep readers on the edge of their seats. The key to building suspense is uncertainty. Readers should be constantly wondering what will happen next, and they should feel a sense of dread or anticipation about the possible outcomes. This can be achieved in many ways, from using cliffhangers at the end of chapters, to withholding information, or setting up high-stakes situations where the characters have a lot to lose.

Understanding Character Conflict

Character conflict is also an essential part of creating tension. This can be conflict between characters, such as a disagreement or rivalry or internal conflict within a character, such as a moral dilemma or fear. Conflict drives a character to act and make decisions, which in turn drives the story forward. It's important to ensure that your character's conflicts are rooted in their personalities and motivations to ensure they feel real and compelling.

Incorporating Themes and Stakes

Lastly, don't forget about the bigger picture. *Themes and stakes* can add depth to your conflict and tension. By tying your conflict to broader themes or issues, you can make your story more resonant and meaningful. And by raising the stakes, you can make the conflict more intense and the tension more palpable. The stakes could be personal, affecting only your character, or they could be much larger, impacting the world or society at large.

Remember, conflict and tension are what keep a story moving, and they're what keeps a reader engaged. So don't be afraid to challenge your characters, throw curveballs, and keep the suspense high. By using these strategies, you'll be able to create a story that is not only exciting but also deeply compelling.

Incorporating Themes and Messages

In the beginning of my bid, I went through a phase where I collected quotes. I don't remember when or why I started, just that I started, and it lasted about three or four years. My people knew this about me and would send me quotes at the end of their letters. One night in particular, I got an envelope from Ma Dukes with maybe five or six pages, front and back, full of quotes. I remember reading over them and looking up at my dorm like *damn, this is powerful*. In that moment I wanted so badly to let them all read some of the quotes, because the same way I needed to hear them, I felt they could use the messages also. This wasn't one of the quotes I received that night, but I read somewhere on a wall in juvenile that *"One's mind once stretched by a new idea never regains its original dimensions,"* which means that once you're exposed to something mentally and get to thinking in a new direction, you'll never see the world exactly the same as you did before you were exposed to that thought.

I went through, circled my favorite quotes in that envelope, and immediately began plotting on a scene in which I could incorporate all of them. I was in the middle of writing *The Hottest Summer Ever,* and as I flipped through, an idea for a scene jumped out at me. It was the scene where the Juvenile Corrections Officer, Ms. Johnson, enters Kush's cell to have a talk and try to get through to her. I wanted to drop some gems in a way that didn't seem forced, and it worked. Till this day, it's a lot of people's favorite scene in the book and it wasn't even originally a part of the manuscript.

In the world of fiction writing, ***incorporating themes and messages*** into your story is essential to create a captivating and thought-provoking narrative. For incarcerated aspiring authors, this endeavor becomes even more crucial as literature offers a powerful means of self-expression and connection with the outside world. Whether you are a fan of urban fiction or exploring other genres, this chapter will guide you on how to identify key themes, develop symbolism, and infuse your story with meaningful messages.

. . .

1. Understanding Themes:

Themes are the underlying ideas, concepts, or issues explored in a work of fiction. They provide depth and resonance to your story, allowing readers to engage with the characters and their struggles on a deeper level. To identify key themes:

A. Reflect on personal experiences: Draw from your own life experiences, observations, and emotions to uncover themes that resonate with you. Consider the challenges, triumphs, and conflicts that have shaped your journey.

B. Explore societal issues: Examine the world around you and the issues that affect your community. Themes can be related to social justice, inequality, personal growth, family dynamics, or any other pertinent topics.

C. Analyze characters and plot: Analyze your character's motivations, conflicts, and relationships. Look for recurring ideas or patterns that emerge throughout your story.

2. Developing Symbolism:

Symbolism is a powerful literary device that adds layers of meaning to your writing. By using symbols, you can convey deeper messages and evoke emotional responses from your readers. Here are some tips for developing symbolism:

A. Objects and settings: Choose objects or settings that hold symbolic significance. For example, a dilapidated building may represent decay or a broken system, while a blooming flower could symbolize hope or resilience.

B. Colors and imagery: Utilize colors and vivid imagery to convey symbolism. For instance, the color *red* might symbolize passion or danger, while a stormy sky could represent turmoil or conflict.

C. Character names: Select names that reflect character traits or symbolic meanings. A protagonist named Grace might represent redemption, while a villain named Shadow could symbolize darkness or deceit.

D. Metaphors and allegories: Incorporate metaphors and allegories to convey abstract concepts. By comparing two unrelated things, you can create a deeper understanding of your themes and messages.

3. Balancing Themes and Storytelling:

While themes and messages are essential, it's crucial to maintain a balance between conveying your ideas and telling an engaging story. Here are a few tips:

A. Character-driven narratives: Develop characters that embody and explore your chosen themes. Through their experiences and growth, you can effectively convey your messages without sacrificing the storytelling aspect.

B. Show, don't tell: Instead of explicitly stating your

themes, allow them to emerge naturally through the actions, dialogue, and relationships of your characters. Show the consequences of certain beliefs or behaviors to engage readers on a deeper level.

C. **Multiple perspectives:** Incorporate diverse viewpoints and perspectives to add complexity to your themes. This allows readers to engage with different sides of an issue and form their own conclusions.

D. **Emotional resonance:** Create emotional connections with your readers by infusing your themes with relatable experiences and universal emotions. This will help your messages resonate and leave a lasting impact.

Remember, the incorporation of themes and messages is a subtle art. Don't force your ideas upon the reader but allow them to discover and interpret the deeper meanings within your story. Here are a few additional tips to consider:

4. Research and Read Widely:

Expand your knowledge and understanding of themes and messages by reading a variety of literature across different genres. Explore both classic and contemporary works to gain insights into how renowned authors incorporate themes into their writing. This exposure will help you refine your own storytelling techniques and develop a unique voice.

5. Seek Feedback and Collaboration:

While incarcerated, it may be challenging to access a broad range of perspectives. However, seek feedback from fellow inmates who share a passion for writing or reading. Engage in writing workshops or book clubs within your facility to exchange ideas, provide constructive criticism, and collaborate on refining your themes and messages.

6. Stay True to Your Voice:

As an aspiring author, it's vital to remain authentic to your voice and experiences. While it's essential to incorporate themes and messages, don't compromise your unique perspective. Use your own background and insights to infuse your writing with an originality that will resonate with readers.

7. Revise and Polish:

Once you have completed a draft of your story, revise and polish it to ensure that your themes and messages are effectively integrated. Consider seeking feedback from trusted friends, family members, or mentors outside of prison who can provide fresh perspectives and constructive criticism. Revise your work accordingly, paying attention to the clarity and impact of your themes.

8. Research Publishing Opportunities:

While incarcerated, it's essential to research publishing opportunities specifically tailored for incarcerated authors. There are organizations and initiatives dedicated to providing a platform for incarcerated writers to share their work. Explore these avenues and consider submitting your manuscripts to literary magazines, anthologies, or online platforms that support incarcerated writers.

Remember, the power of storytelling lies in its ability to transcend physical boundaries. By incorporating themes and messages into your writing, you have the opportunity to connect with readers on a profound level, regardless of your current circumstances. Use this chapter as a guide to develop your story with depth, meaning, and impact, and let your words inspire and empower others, both within and beyond the walls.

Editing and Revising Your Story

Last but certainly not least, as I've spoken on time and time again, *editing and revising* is an essential part of the writing process, and it's important to take the time to review and refine your work.

Writing Your Book

"When I sat down and tried it, it was the most natural thing I did."
— K'wan

<u>Pimp Yo Pen</u>

Welcome to the new found journey of writing your book...or maybe it's not so new. But as the saying goes, *"a one thousand mile journey begins with one step."* So whether you aspire to be a novelist, a memoirist, or a poet, this chapter is dedicated to incarcerated aspiring authors like yourself who are ready to **unleash their creativity and share their stories** with the world. In *How To Publish a Book from Prison*, I aim to provide you with practical guidance and valuable insights to help you navigate the process of writing and ultimately publishing your work.

Writing, in its many forms, has the power to transcend physical boundaries and connect people from all walks of life. Despite your current circumstances, you possess a unique perspective and a wealth of experiences that can captivate readers, stimulate their imagination, and leave a lasting impact. Through the written word, you have the ability to transport your readers to new worlds, evoke emotions, and challenge their perceptions.

Within the next few pages, we will explore various aspects of the writing process that will aid you in crafting your story. We will delve into the importance of creating a solid outline to give your book structure and direction, providing you with a roadmap to guide your narrative. Additionally, we will discuss effective techniques for setting writing goals, helping you establish a clear vision and breaking down how to write a book into manageable steps.

I understand that staying motivated in an environment like prison can be challenging, but just chill. I'm putting you on game about ways to help you maintain your creative spark and overcome obstacles that may arise along the way. Your potential as a writer is endless, and I'm here to support you in your journey towards literary success.

Whether you dream of seeing your book on bookstore shelves, reaching a wide audience, or simply leaving a legacy for future generations, this chapter will equip you with the tools you need to transform your aspirations into reality. It is my hope that by the end of this book, you will not only have a completed manuscript in your hands but also a comprehensive understanding of the publishing industry and the avenues available to you for sharing your work with the world.

Remember, your story matters. Writing has the power to transcend physical confinement and make an impact far beyond the wall. So, let's embark on this transformative journey together and unlock the writer within you. The world is waiting to hear your voice, and I'm here to guide you every step of the way.

Understanding Urban Fiction

Before you start writing your Urban Fiction book, it is essential to **understand the genre**. Urban Fiction is a type of street literature that focuses on the experiences of people living in urban areas. It typically features themes such as street violence, drug trafficking, and gang culture. Urban Fiction is often characterized by its raw, gritty, and realistic portrayal of life in the inner city.

To write a successful Urban Fiction book, you need to immerse yourself in the genre. Read widely in the genre to get a sense of the themes, characters, and writing style that are prevalent. You can also watch movies or TV shows set in the inner city to get a visual representation of the world you are writing about...but for those of us who've lived it and come from that, this should be a genre you dominate.

"Urban fiction to me is like the black stories of the nasty streets entwined with the minds of all the hood ways and choices," Chris Green, author of *Atlantastan: Chaos City,* says. *"It's a guide for most who can't understand our culture because we can give you so many different scenarios of black excellence through any mindset: a negative or a positive. See, urban fiction can make your adrenaline boil, or it can cause it to simmer. It can make you excited, but at the same time, cause you to grow sad. It's a world of black minds on our suffering and pain and sometimes an outlet for the urban novelist to express how they see life."*

In essence, Urban Fiction serves as a powerful conduit for the voices of those who navigate the complexities of inner-city life. It captures the raw intensity of their experiences, blending the harsh realities of the streets with moments of resilience and hope. As an urban fiction writer, your task is to authentically portray these multifaceted narratives, creating characters and stories that resonate with readers on a profound level. Whether you're drawing from personal experience or extensive research, your goal is to contribute to this rich literary tapestry with authenticity and respect. By doing so, you not only entertain but also enlighten, offering a glimpse into the diverse and dynamic world of urban life.

. . .

Developing Your Characters

Strong characters are essential to any book, but they are particularly important in Urban Fiction. Your characters should be complex, multi-dimensional, and relatable. They should have flaws, strengths, and a backstory that informs their actions and motivations.

To **develop your characters**, start by creating character profiles. These should include information about their background, personality, motivations, and goals. You should also think about how your characters will interact with each other and the world around them.

We spoke more in depth about this in Chapter 2.

Setting the Scene

The **setting** is another important element of Fiction. Your setting should be authentic and immersive, transporting your readers to the world you are writing about.

To set the scene, you need to do your research. If you are writing about a specific city or neighborhood, you would generally want to visit it. One of the dopest things to me about Eric Jerome Dickey's books was how after the story, he would always have an author's note, which was always written while he was in a scene in the book in whatever city or country the setting of the book was in. He visited the places he was writing about and stayed there until he finished the project. Whether it was London, South America, or wherever...he would go, and a dope ass story would be written.

Our situation may hinder us from going to different places physically, but we can always talk to people who live there and learn about their experiences. You can also use maps and other tools to get a sense of the layout and geography of the place. Pay attention to the small details that make a location unique: the way the air smells, the pace of life, the sounds that fill the air, and the architecture that defines the skyline. If your setting is historical, read books or watch documentaries about the era. Look at old maps, photographs, and other primary sources that can give you a sense of what life was like during that time.

When writing a fictional world, the research involves creating a setting that is consistent and believable within its own context. Draw inspiration from real-world cultures, climates, and ecosystems to make your world compelling. Consider the rules of your world, whether they pertain to magic, technology, social structure, or the laws of physics, and ensure they are clear and consistently applied throughout your story.

As you write the description of your setting, remember that it's not necessary to include every detail you've researched or imagined. Instead, include details that enhance the mood, develop the plot, or reveal something about the characters. Use sensory details to help the reader experience the setting as if they were there but avoid overwhelming them with too much information at once. The key is to sprinkle details throughout your narrative to maintain the flow of the story while enriching the reader's experience.

For example, if your character is walking through a crowded marketplace, you might focus on all the sounds: vendors shouting, the clink of coins, the sizzle of food cooking. If your character is entering a library, you might describe the smell of old books, the hushed whispers, and the vastness of the space filled with countless bookshelves.

Remember also to consider how the setting affects the characters and the plot. The setting can act almost as a character itself, shaping the lives and decisions of those within it. A harsh, unforgiving landscape might make life difficult for your characters, influencing their development and the challenges they face. A thriving city with a rich cultural life might offer opportunities for intrigue and complex social interactions.

Lastly, keep in mind the time of day and weather, as these can also greatly impact the atmosphere of your scene. I get countless manuscripts where the characters are outside and active and I don't even know the weather because it's never mentioned. The reason that this is done most of the time is because we as the writers see the scene in our heads and focus on the action, forgetting that the reader can only see what we see if we put it in the story. Remember, the same location can feel entirely different in the soft light of dawn as opposed to the harsh shadows of midday, in a gentle spring drizzle versus a fierce winter blizzard.

By thoroughly researching and thoughtfully incorporating details, you can create a setting that breathes life into your story and captivates your readers' imaginations.

Creating a Compelling Plot

Another critical element of Fiction, or any fiction, is a *compelling plot*. Your plot should be engaging, fast-paced, and full of twists and turns. It should keep your readers on the edge of their seats and leave them wanting more.

To create a compelling plot, start by outlining your story. Identify the key plot points and how they will connect. Think about the conflicts and obstacles your characters will face and how they will overcome them. You should also consider the pacing of your story. Your plot should move at a brisk pace but not so fast that your readers can't keep up.

Creating A Story Outline

As you embark on the journey of writing your book within the confines of prison, it's essential to recognize that every author's approach to storytelling is unique. Some writers prefer to let their creativity flow unbounded, writing as they go and allowing the narrative to unfold organically.

Others meticulously research and compile notes before penning a single word or write scenes out of order to be pieced together later like a literary jigsaw puzzle. There are those who swear by the "snowflake method," gradually expanding a single sentence into a full-blown novel, and those who engage in extensive character development exercises to fully understand their cast before setting them in motion. Yet, amidst this diversity of methods, one technique stands out for its ability to provide structure and direction, especially in an environment where resources and time may be limited: *creating a solid story outline.*

An outline serves as a roadmap for your narrative, a skeleton on which to flesh out your story. It's particularly important when your writing conditions are challenging, as it keeps you focused and ensures every precious moment dedicated to your craft moves you closer to your endpoint. Here's how to create an effective outline for your book:

1. **Conceptualize Your Core Idea:** Begin with your central concept or question. This is the seed from which your story will grow – a clear, concise statement that captures the essence of your narrative.

2. **Establish Your Premise:** Expand your core idea into a premise, which includes the setting, characters, and basic situation of your story. This

should be a short paragraph summarizing the overall plot.

3. **Define Your Characters:** Before delving into plot points, take time to outline your key characters. Who are they? What do they want? What obstacles do they face? How will they change throughout the story? These profiles will inform your plot's progression.

4. **Plot Your Story Arc:** Break down your narrative into the three-act structure: Setup, Confrontation, and Resolution. Sketch out the major events that will occur in each section. Your outline should include the inciting incident, rising action, climax, falling action, and denouement.

5. **Detail Scenes and Chapters:** Further break down each act into scenes or chapters. What happens in each? What's the goal of each scene? What information is revealed? How does it move the story forward? Write a brief description for each scene or chapter in your outline.

6. **Incorporate Subplots:** If your story includes subplots, weave these into your main outline, ensuring they complement the main story arc and contribute to character development and thematic depth.

7. **Plan for Character Development:** Outline how your characters will evolve throughout the story.

What lessons will they learn? How will their goals and motivations shift?

8. **Foreshadowing and Themes:** Identify any elements of foreshadowing or recurring themes you want to include. Decide where and how these will appear throughout your story.

9. **Revise Your Outline:** An outline is a living document. As you begin writing, you may discover new ideas or decide to take your story in a different direction. Regularly revisiting and revising your outline will ensure it remains a useful guide.

10. **Seek Feedback:** If possible, share your outline with trusted fellow writers, mentors, or educators in your facility. Constructive feedback can help refine your roadmap before you begin the drafting process.

Remember, outlining is not about creating a rigid structure that constrains your creativity, but rather about giving you a clear direction to channel it. As you're working within the unique circumstances of prison, having this structure is even more crucial—it's a tool to manage your limited resources efficiently, both in terms of time and materials.

11. **Break It Down:** Once you have your overall outline, break it down further into manageable writing goals. This might mean setting out what you aim to achieve each week

or month. Given the restrictions you might face in prison, such as limited writing time or interruptions, having smaller, achievable targets can help maintain your motivation and ensure steady progress.

12. **Adaptability:** Your outline should be detailed enough to guide you, but flexible enough to allow for changes as your story evolves. It's common for characters to take on lives of their own or for unexpected plot twists to emerge as you delve deeper into the writing process. Embrace these moments of inspiration—they often lead to the most compelling narratives.

13. **Consistency and Continuity:** An outline also helps you maintain consistency and continuity in your story. As you might have writing interruptions due to prison routines, returning to your work can be made easier with a clear outline to remind you of where you are in the story and what needs to come next.

14. **Resource Management:** In prison, your access to research materials or writing aids may be limited. Your outline can help you identify areas where you need more information, allowing you to focus your requests or research efforts more effectively.

15. **Legal Considerations:** Consider any legal implications of your story, especially if it's based on real events or people. An outline can help you identify potential legal issues early on, such as the need to change names or details to protect privacy or avoid libel.

16. End with a Vision: Finally, conclude your outline with a vision for your manuscript's completion. Having a clear end goal can serve as a source of inspiration and a reminder of why you embarked on this journey. Visualize yourself holding the finished book, and let this image drive you through the challenges of writing within the prison system.

By investing time in creating a well-thought-out story outline, you're not only setting a solid foundation for your narrative, but you're also equipping yourself with a strategic plan that can navigate the constraints of your environment. This outline will be your companion and guide, steering you toward the ultimate goal of publishing your book and sharing your unique voice with the world beyond the prison walls.

Setting Writing Goals

Embarking on the journey to write and publish a book from prison presents a unique set of challenges and constraints. However, these can be overcome with determination, clarity of vision, and a strategic approach to goal setting. *Effective goal setting* is the backbone of successful writing, transforming the monumental task of authorship into a series of achievable steps. This section will guide you through the process of setting clear, actionable writing goals that will keep you motivated and on track throughout your literary quest.

1. Define Your Purpose.

Begin by asking yourself why you want to write a book. Your purpose could be to tell your story, share your expertise, inspire others, or simply to leave a legacy. Understanding your 'why' will fuel your determination and help you stay committed when the process becomes challenging.

2. Create a Vision Statement.

Draft a vision statement that encapsulates the essence of your book. This should be a clear and concise declaration of what you aim to achieve with your writing. Think of it as the guiding star for your project, keeping you focused on the end goal.

3. Break It Down.

Writing a book is a marathon, not a sprint. Break down your project into smaller, more manageable goals. Consider the following components:

A. Research: What topics do you need to explore? What can you access within your current environment?

B. Outline: How will your book be structured? What are the key chapters or sections?

C. Writing: Set word count targets for each writing session or week.

D. Editing: Plan for reviewing and revising your manuscript.

E. Networking: Think about how you can connect with other writers, editors, and potential mentors through available channels.

4. Set SMART Goals.

Ensure your goals are Specific, Measurable, Achievable, Relevant, and Time-bound (SMART). For instance, rather than setting a vague goal like "work on my book," a SMART goal would be "write 500 words each weekday morning."

5. Establish a Routine.

Consistency is key. Set aside dedicated time for writing and stick to it as best as you can. Even if you can only manage a small amount of time each day, the cumulative effect of regular writing will be significant.

6. Use Milestones.

Celebrate small victories by setting milestones. This

could be completing a chapter, reaching a certain word count, or finishing your first draft. Acknowledge these achievements to maintain your motivation.

7. Adapt and Overcome.

Incarceration involves unpredictability. Your routine may be disrupted, resources may become unavailable, or you may face other setbacks. Be prepared to adapt your goals and methods as needed. Flexibility is a vital aspect of resilience.

8. Visualize Success.

Regularly visualize the moment you achieve your goal of not only completing your book but also holding the published work in your hands. This powerful mental practice can help you stay energized and committed to your writing journey.

9. Record Your Progress.

Keep a writing log or journal to track your progress. Documenting your journey will not only help you stay on course but also provide a sense of accomplishment as you fill pages with evidence of your hard work.

By setting and pursuing well-crafted goals, you'll not only progress in writing your book but also develop a sense of purpose and self-efficacy that transcends the confines of your current environment. Writing a book from prison is not simply about reaching the end; it's about the transformation that occurs within you as an author during the process. Remember that each word you write is a step closer to your goal, and each goal achieved is a testament to your dedication and strength.

10. Re-evaluate Regularly.

Goals are not set in stone. As you progress with your writing, take time to reflect on your goals. Are they still relevant? Do you need to increase your daily word count to meet your deadline? Are there new challenges you need to account for? Regularly re-evaluating your goals ensures they remain aligned with your vision and current circumstances.

11. Manage Expectations.

Be realistic about what you can achieve within the confines of prison. Access to resources and support may be limited, and you will likely have to navigate institutional policies and restrictions. Setting ambitious yet realistic goals will help you avoid frustration and stay motivated.

12. Leverage Resources.

Make the most of the resources available to you. This might include prison libraries, books (like this one your reading), other people (in the publishing industry, with knowledge of the publishing industry, or someone dedicated to helping you with what you're striving to accomplish), educational programs, or writing workshops (if your prison has any). If you have access to a mentorship program, take advantage of it to help you refine your goals and writing strategies.

13. Plan for Post-Completion Steps.

While your current focus is on writing the book, don't neglect to set goals for the steps that follow completion, such as revising, submitting to a publisher or exploring self-publishing options. Having a plan for these next stages will give you a clearer path to follow once your manuscript is finished.

14. Stay Connected with Your Support Network.

Maintain communication with your support network, whether that's a writing group within the prison or contacts on the outside. Sharing your goals and progress can provide you with a sense of community and support that is invaluable when writing in such challenging circumstances.

By setting thoughtful and tailored writing goals, you can

navigate the complexities of writing and publishing a book from prison. These goals will serve as your roadmap, guiding you through each chapter of your writing journey until you reach the ultimate destination: a published author with a story that can resonate beyond the walls that currently contain you. Keep pushing forward, one word at a time, and believe in the power of your voice and your story.

Igniting Your Creative Flame Behind Bars

Staying motivated in the trenches can most definitely test the human spirit, but don't let that deter you. Look at it as a challenge to rise above. There's a well of creative energy inside you, enough to create a spark that can ignite a transformative fire, capable of turning the darkest of cells into the brightest of workshops. This section is a brief dedication to *fanning those flames* and equipping you with the practical strategies you need to maintain your creative drive and navigate any obstacle that stands in your path.

First, understand that your current environment, no matter how restrictive, *does not* define your potential as a writer. Within your mind lies a boundless universe, ripe for exploration and expression through the written word. I believe in your potential, and it is my commitment to support you as you journey toward literary success through the words on these pages.

To keep the creative spark alive, you must establish a

routine that incorporates time for writing, reading, and reflection. Consistency breeds progress, and progress will fuel your motivation. Create a schedule that respects the strictness of your environment, but also sets aside solo moments for your craft.

Engage with literature that inspires you. Books are conduits of freedom, transporting you to worlds unchained by physical barriers. Draw inspiration from the stories and voices that resonate with your soul and let them guide your own narrative journey. I always say that the best authors are avid readers, and even if you're an Urban author, I still think it would be a good idea to be a voracious reader of other genres as well.

Embrace the power of education. Take advantage of any programs, courses (ex: Stratford Career Institute's Creative Writing course), or resources available to you, as they can provide the tools to refine your craft and expand your knowledge. Learning is a lifelong endeavor, and every new insight is a steppingstone toward your goal.

Build a support network. Connect with fellow inmates (they don't have to be at your prison) who share your passion for writing, along with understanding correctional staff and outside mentors. Collaboration and feedback are invaluable, as they offer new perspectives and encouragement.

Above all, view every challenge as an opportunity for growth. The obstacles inherent to your situation can become the very source of your greatest strength as a writer. For example, the challenge of me publishing from prison has allowed me to write this very book. Write about your experiences, emotions, and observations. They are unique to you and can forge a powerful connection with readers beyond the prison walls.

Remember, your journey as an author is not a sprint but a marathon. There will be days when the words flow effortlessly and others when they seem trapped behind the bars of your mind. It is in those tougher moments that your commitment to your craft is most crucial. *Perseverance* is the hallmark of any successful writer, and your current circumstances can become the crucible in which your determination is forged.

In Chapter 10, we will provide you with actionable steps to keep your creative fires burning. Together, we will navigate this path, for the world awaits the stories only you can tell. As you step into your writing career, do so with unwavering resolve and the knowledge that every word you write is a step closer to the freedom of expression and the success you so rightly deserve.

Editing Your Book

"A good editor is definitely important to polish your writing, but at the end of the day, you are the storyteller."

—K'wan

Understanding the Editing Process

Before you start editing your book, it is essential to understand the editing process. *Editing* involves revising and refining your manuscript to improve its overall quality. This includes fixing grammar and spelling errors, improving sentence structure, and enhancing the rhythm, flow, and coherence of your story. You're probably thinking what I thought the first time I heard those phrases applied to writing: *A book has rhythm and flow?*

The answer is *yes*. It does, but in a much different way than rap. You ever read a book that you couldn't put down? That book more than likely flowed well. There are certain things like not having the same words in a following sentence, balancing out using a character's name versus using a pronoun, not consecutively beginning a sentence the same way, etc. The reader will not be aware of why they can't put the book down, but as an author, it's something that you should be aware of.

To edit your book effectively, you need to be able to view your work objectively. This means stepping back from your writing and approaching it with a critical eye. You should also be prepared to make tough decisions about what to keep and what to cut, as well as being open to feedback from others.

Identifying Problem Areas

Once you have a solid understanding of the editing process, the next step is to *identify problem areas* in your manuscript. These can include issues with plot, character development, pacing, or dialogue.

To identify problem areas, start by reading through your manuscript from beginning to end. Take notes on any issues you encounter and make note of any sections that feel weak or disjointed. You can also ask a trusted friend or writing partner to provide feedback on your manuscript. I have to say this, though. Make sure this person that you receive feedback from is someone who's name would hold weight on the subject at hand. That means don't have Shawty Black, who doesn't really read like that, read your manuscript and tell you it's a go, because there's a strong possibility it could be a *no*. Find an honest avid reader, preferably someone who's *stand up* enough to give harsh feedback when it's needed. Another thing, too...don't be sensitive. Keep an open mind and remember that there's always room for improvement.

Fixing Grammar and Spelling Errors

One of the most basic tasks of editing is *fixing grammar and spelling errors*. This includes correcting typos, ensuring proper punctuation, and fixing any grammatical mistakes.

To fix grammar and spelling errors, you can use a variety of tools. Many word processing programs have built-in spell checkers and grammar checkers that can help you identify and correct errors. You can also use online tools such as Grammarly or Hemingway Editor to help you identify and fix errors.

Improving Sentence Structure

Another important aspect of editing is *improving sentence*

structure. This includes ensuring that your sentences are clear, concise, and well-constructed.

To improve sentence structure, start by reading your manuscript *out loud*. This can help you identify any sentences that are awkward or difficult to read. You can also break up long sentences into shorter, more manageable chunks, and vary sentence length to keep your writing engaging.

Enhancing the Rhythm, Flow, and Coherence of Your Story

Finally, editing involves **enhancing the flow and coherence of your story**. This means ensuring that your story moves smoothly from beginning to end, with all the pieces fitting together seamlessly. I mentioned some of the ways to do so at the beginning of this section, but there are a few other things to look for when it comes to rhythm and flow. It just takes practice. Overtime, you'll develop a feel for it.

To begin, start by examining the structure of your manuscript. Make sure that your story has a clear beginning, middle, and end, and that all the pieces fit together logically. You can also use tools such as storyboards or outlines to help you map out your story and ensure that it flows smoothly.

Enhancing the rhythm, flow, and coherence of your story is critical to engage your readers and ensure they remain invested from start to finish. For incarcerated aspiring authors, this process is even more crucial as you may not have easy access to resources, feedback, or the internet for research. Here's how you can refine your manuscript to achieve a seamless narrative:

Things to Avoid to Improve Flow:

1. **Repetitive Sentence Structure:** Varying sentence length and structure prevents monotony. Don't start every sentence the same way and avoid using the same sentence patterns repeatedly.

2. **Overuse of a Word:** If a word appears too often, it loses its impact. Look for synonyms or rephrase sentences to avoid repetition. I recommend you order in a good Thesaurus and Dictionary of you don't have one. This will help you come up with a variety of different words and help you to not use them out of context. Trust me...it happens a lot more than it should.

3. **Starting Sentences with "After":** This can lead to a series of sentences that feel passive or secondary to the main action. Instead, try to find active ways to describe events.

4. **Overusing Adverbs:** Adverbs (words typically ending in -ly) can clutter your writing. Strong verbs often eliminate the need for an adverb.

5. **Excessive Flashbacks:** While useful for providing backstory, too many flashbacks can disrupt the narrative flow. Use them sparingly and ensure they serve a clear purpose.

6. **Info-dumping:** Introducing too much background information at once can overwhelm the reader. Spread exposition throughout the narrative, weaving it into action and dialogue.

7. **Passive Voice:** Passive sentences can make your writing seem indirect. Use *active voice* to make sentences clearer and more dynamic.

Techniques to Enhance Story Flow:

1. **Transition Words and Phrases:** These help to link sentences and paragraphs smoothly, guiding the reader from one idea to another.

2. **Chapter Breaks and White Space:** Use these to give readers a pause and to signal shifts in time, setting, or point of view.

3. **Dialogue:** Natural-sounding dialogue can break up long paragraphs and add immediacy to your story.

4. **Subheadings within Chapters:** If your story is non-linear or involves complex information,

subheadings can help organize thoughts and guide the reader.

5. **Rhythm in Writing:** Pay attention to the rhythm of your sentences. Read your work aloud to hear how it flows.

Detailed Breakdown of Techniques:

1. **Structure and Pacing:** Your story should have a discernible beginning, middle, and end. The beginning sets up the conflict; the middle lets it unfold; and the end resolves it. Pacing is how quickly the story progresses. Mix up longer, more descriptive passages with short, punchy scenes to keep the reader engaged.

2. **Paragraph Structure:** Each paragraph should deal with a single idea or action. This helps in creating a logical flow. Transition sentences at the end of paragraphs can help to lead into the next topic or scene.

3. **Character's Actions and Reactions:** Ensure that character's actions and reactions are believable and contribute to the narrative. This adds to the story's rhythm by creating a cause-and-effect chain that readers can follow.

4. **Motifs and Symbols:** Repeating motifs or symbols can create a sense of rhythm and unity within the story. This doesn't mean repeating the same word, but rather revisiting an idea or theme from different angles.

5. **Varied Sentence Length:** Mixing short and long sentences keeps the reader's interest and can be used to control pacing. Short sentences speed up the action, while longer ones slow it down and add detail.

6. **Use of Sensory Details:** The five senses can be powerful tools in setting the scene and enhancing the flow. Describe how things look, sound, smell, feel, and taste to immerse the reader in the world you're creating.

7. **Clarity and Conciseness:** Be clear and concise in your writing. Don't let your message get lost in overly complex sentences or jargon.

8. **Feedback:** While access to internet or writer's groups may be limited, feedback is still vital. Share your work with fellow inmates or prison staff who are willing to read it and offer their thoughts.

9. **Revision:** Don't be afraid to cut or rewrite parts that don't work. Sometimes, what you remove improves the overall flow of the story more than what you add.

. . .

Remember, writing within the confines of prison means finding creativity within limitations. Use your environment, experiences, and the time available to you to refine your story, focus on the craft, and pour your unique voice onto the page. Your story has the potential to resonate powerfully, not despite your circumstances, but because of them.

More on editing in Chapter 6.

Finding a Publisher

"The urban fiction genre may not be hip hop, but it's definitely like the rap game and drug game. Representation is so important."
—Danielle Santiago

Though you can sign a traditional publishing contract, navigating the process from behind the wall requires a different approach than traditional publishing. In this chapter, we'll explore the various options available to incarcerated writers, including self-publishing, traditional publishing, and hybrid publishing. We'll discuss the pros and cons of each approach and I'll give you the rundown on maneuvering in the publishing process from behind bars. We'll also cover the process of finding a publisher, including how to research publishers, how to write a query letter, how to prepare your manuscript for submission, and touch briefly on important topics such as copyright law, distribution, and marketing. However, I won't go too hard on these due to them being discussed in depth in other chapters in this book.

Being Persistent and Patient

Aight, let's keep it 1K. You're behind the wall, your dreams cracked up against the cold concrete, and you're trying to make sense of it all. You're thinking about writing, about penning those thoughts that keep you up at night, those stories that burn inside you like a furnace. But you're also thinking about the world out there, the publishing industry, and how it might look at someone like you. I ain't gone cap you down. It ain't gonna be easy, but it's possible, and the keys are *persistence and patience.*

First off, know this: The publishing industry is not a charity. They're in business to make money, looking for stories that sell, and they don't care where those stories come from. If you can spin a tale that grabs the reader by the collar and won't let go, they'll want you. The thing is, getting to that point takes time. It takes practice. It takes persistence.

Think about your favorite authors, the ones who penned

those gritty urban tales that resonate with your own experience. Do you think they got there overnight? No. They wrote, they scraped, they hustled. They faced rejection after rejection, but they never gave up. They were persistent.

And you have to be the same. You have to keep writing, keep refining, keep pushing. Every word you write is a step closer to your goal. Every story you finish is another notch on your belt. And remember, you're not alone. There are organizations out there that work with incarcerated writers, helping them to hone their craft and get their work out into the world.

Take Jimmy Santiago Baca for example. He went to prison, didn't even know how to read, but he taught himself, started writing, and became one of the most respected poets in America. Or Chester Himes, who started writing while doing a stretch in Ohio State Penitentiary and ended up penning the *Harlem Detective* series.

But here's the other side of the coin: Patience. The publishing industry moves slow, slower than molasses in January. It can take years to get a book deal, and even longer to actually *see* your book on the shelves. But don't let that discourage you. Use that time to your advantage. Keep writing, keep learning, keep growing. Make every day count.

Remember, your situation is a part of your story, but it's not the whole tale. You're more than the bars that hold you, more than the mistakes you've made. You're a writer, a storyteller, a dream spinner. And if you're persistent, if you're patient, you can turn those dreams into reality.

As the great Maya Angelou, a phenomenal black author and poet, once said, *"You may encounter many defeats, but you must not be defeated. In fact, it may be necessary to encounter the defeats, so you can know who you are, what you can rise from, and how you can still come out of it."*

So, keep your pen moving, your spirit unbroken, and let your voice soar above those prison walls. Because your story is worth telling, and the world is waiting to hear it.

Finding a publisher for your book can be hell, especially if you are doing it from prison. However, it is not impossible. Once I completed my first novel and got it typed, I began writing EVERYBODY! I had been ordering and reading books by authors and companies that you probably haven't even heard of. I would read the book and if I liked the cover, and the story had little to no errors, I would go to the copyright page, write down the publisher's address, and write them. Would I get any response? No. But what I didn't know about then was *Submission Guidelines*. I'll share a story on that in this chapter.

All in all, with the right mindset, knowledge, and tools, you can find a publisher that will help you bring your book to market.

. . .

Understanding the Publishing Industry

Publishing is not merely a glittering façade; it's an intricate process that surpasses the simple act of committing words to paper with aspirations of landing on the bestseller list. But don't be intimidated. Every industry operates by a set of rules; the publishing sector is no exception. It's a matter of mastering these rules, navigating smartly, and keeping your focus on your goals.

Understanding the types of publishing available is crucial. There's traditional publishing, where a publishing house acquires the rights to your manuscript. They possess the authority to edit your work and may alter the title you're attached to. They handle the publishing expenses while you receive a cut of the sales, for some genres typically through an advance and subsequent royalties. Securing a traditional publishing deal can feel akin to winning the lottery—challenging but not beyond reach.

Alternatively, self-publishing affords you more control. You make decisions about the book's cover, title, and pricing, and you retain the profits. However, this autonomy means you are also responsible for the costs associated with publishing, marketing, and distribution.

For those navigating these waters from incarceration, know that it *is* possible. You'll need to rely heavily on a trusted contact outside—a pen pal, family member, or friend —to act as your liaison to the publishing world.

Start with the resources at hand; prison library books on

the publishing industry, though potentially dated, can still provide foundational knowledge. Titles such as "The Business of Writing: Understanding the Publishing Industry" by Jennifer Lyons or "How to Get Your Book Published" by Jane Friedman can be invaluable. Additionally, the annual "Writer's Market" is a directory of publishing opportunities. Stratford Career Institute gifts you the latest edition for free when you graduate the course, or you can have your external contact secure the latest edition and share with you the relevant excerpts or summaries...or send it to you, if possible.

Your external assistant can further your research by *investigating* publishers who specialize in your genre, such as urban fiction. They can gather submission guidelines, types of works sought, and contact information for you to review.

A literary agent can be instrumental in bridging the gap between you and potential publishers. You don't necessarily need one, and they're hardly used in Urban Fiction these days. However, for the sake of information, I felt it best if I touched bases on it. They will pitch your book, negotiate deals, and manage contracts. To attract an agent's attention, you'll need to craft a compelling query letter and synopsis that highlight the potential of your work to stand out in the marketplace.

Above all, continue to write. Each narrative you weave is a stride toward realizing your vision. Although you may be physically restrained, your creativity need not be. Allow your words and stories to transcend your confines.

The publishing industry is formidable, but it's not insurmountable with determination, resilience, and strategic planning. Keep in mind, the essence of the game is constant; it's the players who vary. And you, as an incarcerated aspiring author, are indeed *a player*. Prepare to engage fully in the work ahead.

To gain a comprehensive understanding of the publishing industry, one must engage in thorough research. Study literature about the sector and seek insights from published authors. This foundational knowledge will equip you to navigate the industry more effectively and to align your work with what publishers are actively seeking.

Identifying Potential Publishers

Once you have a solid understanding of the publishing industry, the next step is to *identify potential publishers* for your book. There are many publishers that specialize in Urban Fiction, so it is important to find one that is the right fit for your book.

To identify potential publishers, start by researching publishers that specialize in the genre you're writing. Urban Fiction. You can find this information online or by talking to other writers in the genre. Once you have a list of potential publishers, research each one to learn more about their submission guidelines, the types of books they publish, and their reputation in the industry.

. . .

Preparing Your Submission

Once you have identified potential publishers, the next step is to *prepare your submission*. This includes writing a compelling query letter, preparing a synopsis of your book, and ensuring that your manuscript is polished and error-free.

Now, pay attention cause this information is going to save you a lot of time and effort. I wasn't so lucky. As I mentioned earlier, when I completed my first novel and got it typed, I began writing every publishing company I had written down from the copyright page of almost every Urban Fiction, Urban Romance, and Street Lit book I'd saved for almost a year. I wrote Wahida Clark, NVision Publishing, G-Street Chronicles, Black Destiny Publishing, Lockdown Publications, Kensington Books, Urban Books, Cartel Publications, Cash Money Content — all to receive no response. I wrote Tyler Perry and Steve Harvey; I even wrote T.I. and Waka Flocka in an attempt to convince them to start a publishing branch of their label and let me be the face of it. I was thinking Hustle Gang Publishing or Brick Squad Publications. Sounds funny now, but I was dead ass serious. Pulling straws, yes, but all I knew was I had to do something. I was never afraid to dream big or bet on myself. At some point in life, you have to ask yourself if you're aiming too high and missing or are you aiming too low and hitting.

I kept going, kept reading up on the publishing industry, and among other things, two recurring phrases kept standing out to me, one of which was *Submission Guidelines.* The more I thought about the phrase, the more I realized that it was basically rules for submitting something, and because it kept popping up in things related to the industry, I figured there must be a certain way I had to go about giving companies my book, and I was right. I had my people google *Submission Guidelines* and come to find out, every company has a specific way your manuscript must be submitted for you to even be considered for publishing. And get this, right along with that, many blogs and books I read also mentioned that *silence* was the new rejection, which means that if you don't hear nothing back, you already know what it is. That explained why I hadn't heard from anyone.

My approach had been all wrong. Companies don't want you to send them a letter introducing yourself, talking about what you got going on, how long you been locked up, how you're trying to write books to raise money for your lawyer so you can get home to your family, how good your book is, or how all your friends and family say you should be published. They don't care. It makes you look unprofessional and inex-perienced, which to them may mean that you're a potential headache because you're unfamiliar with the publishing process; that means you'll be extra work, because you've never released a title, which in turn means you have no following and therefore, ultimately, may not be worth the investment. Or you just may flat out don't know how to write.

Either way, it isn't good. Avoid this. Visit the website of the companies you're considering as your future publishing home, go to their *Submission Guidelines* page, and submit your work accordingly.

To prepare your submission, start by researching the submission guidelines for each publisher on your list. Follow these guidelines carefully, as failure to do so can result in your submission being rejected. Craft a compelling query letter that highlights the key elements of your book and entices the publisher to read more. Prepare a synopsis of your book that provides a brief overview of the plot, characters, and themes. Finally, ensure that your manuscript is polished and error-free, as this will increase your chances of getting your book published.

Networking and Building Relationships

Building a network and fostering relationships are crucial steps in the journey to getting your book published, even from within the confines of prison. While your situation presents unique challenges, there are still actionable steps you can take to connect with the outside literary world and lay the groundwork for your publishing aspirations.

To begin, leverage the resources available to you. Many prisons offer educational programs, including writing workshops, which can be a valuable space to hone your craft and discuss your work with fellow inmate writers. Participation in these programs can serve as a cornerstone for your literary education and provide a supportive community of like-minded individuals.

If you have access to a prison library, use it to your advantage. Read widely within your genre to understand current trends and identify potential gaps in the market that your writing could fill. Books and literary magazines can also be a source of information about the publishing industry, and they might even contain interviews and advice from authors and agents.

In terms of reaching out beyond the prison walls, consider enlisting the help of a trusted outside assistant – a friend, family member, or volunteer – who can act as your liaison in the literary world. They can attend writing conferences and workshops on your behalf, gathering information, making connections, and even representing your interests to agents and publishers. They can also join writing groups and online forums, sharing your work (with your permission), and building a network of contacts who might be interested in your writing.

Social media platforms such as Facebook, Twitter, Instagram, TikTok, and LinkedIn are invaluable tools for connecting with authors, agents, and publishers. Although you may not have direct access to these platforms, your assistant can create profiles for you and manage them responsibly. They can follow authors in your genre, engage with their content, and help promote their work. This kind of literary citizenship creates goodwill within the community and can lead to mutual support, even increasing the visibility of your own work.

Your assistant can also help you establish a simple author website or blog, where you can share samples of your writing, updates about your journey, and your thoughts on various literary topics. This online presence can serve as a portfolio for your work and a point of contact for interested parties.

Lastly, consider reaching out to nonprofit organizations that focus on writing and education for incarcerated individuals. These organizations may have programs that can assist you with resources, mentorship, or connections to industry professionals.

By being proactive and utilizing these strategies with the help of an outside assistant, you can build a bridge to the literary community and take significant strides towards publishing your book, even from behind bars. Remember: your current circumstances do not define your future potential. Your voice and story matter, and there are people in the literary world ready to hear them.

Chapter 6

Self-Publishing

"If you aren't in the top 1%, self-publishing is your only option. If you are in the top 1%, self-publishing is your best option. There is no case where I recommend someone BEGIN their writing career with a query letter. None."
- High Howey

If you're unable to find a traditional publisher, *self-publishing* is another option. In this chapter, we'll explore the different ways to self-publish your book, including how to choose a platform, how to format your book, and how to market your book.

. . .

The Literary Mixtape

The world of urban fiction is a thriving subgenre of literature that has captured the attention of readers across the globe. With its gritty realism, relatable characters, and hard-hitting themes, urban fiction has become a go-to for readers looking for stories that tackle tough issues in a way that is both entertaining and thought-provoking.

For inmates who are looking to express themselves creatively and share their stories with the world, self-publishing can be an excellent option. Self-publishing allows writers to bypass traditional publishing channels and put their work directly in the hands of readers. It's **the publishing equivalent of dropping a mixtape.**

It's a lot simpler than people think and it's easier than ever. The process is simple: *write the book, name the book, edit the book, get a cover, secure a legitimate ISBN and barcode, typeset the book, and upload it to whichever platform you choose to distribute your books through.* In my opinion Amazon is the most user friendly, but there are other platforms out there such as LuLu, Book Baby, and (the O.G of them all) IngramSpark.

Regardless of which one you decide to go with, be sure to do your own homework on the pros and cons of each and make an informed decision based off which platform would be the most conducive to your publishing goals.

.   .   .

Unlocking the Power of a Title: The Key to Your Book's Success

Writing a book is an *art form*. It is a unique way for you to express your thoughts, ideas, and experiences. Yet, the way you present this masterpiece to the world is equally important. This is where **the title** of your book comes into play. The title is, in essence, the first impression readers will have of your work. It's like the cover of your book – it needs to draw people in, pique their curiosity, and give them a hint of what lies within the pages.

Why are Titles Important?

Titles are crucial for several reasons:

1. **First Impressions:** Much like people, books are often judged by their initial appearance. The title is the first thing a potential reader sees. A compelling, intriguing title can draw readers in, while a dull or confusing one can turn them away.

2. **Reflects the Content:** The title should give a glimpse of what the book is about. It doesn't have to give everything away, but it should convey the main theme or subject of the book. This gives readers an idea of what to expect, helping to attract those who might be interested in the topic.

3. **Memorability:** An effective title sticks in the mind. It's the tagline that readers will remember and use to recommend the book to others. A catchy, memorable title can significantly boost word-of-mouth promotion.

4. **Search ability:** In the age of digital self-publishing, your book isn't just competing on the shelves, but in online searches as well. A well-chosen title that includes key words related to your book's content can help it show up in search results, increasing its visibility.

The Art of Crafting a Title

Crafting a title requires a balance of creativity and strategy. It should be intriguing yet clear, unique but not haphazard. Here are some strategies to help you craft a powerful title:

1. **Keep It Short and Simple:** Long titles can be difficult to remember and may confuse potential readers. Aim for simplicity and clarity.

2. **Use Powerful Language:** Words that evoke strong emotions or vivid imagery can make your title stand out and stick in the reader's mind.

3. **Relate to the Theme or Plot:** Your title should be relevant to your book's content. It could be a significant phrase, symbol, or theme from your book.

4. **Consider Your Audience:** Think about who you're writing for. What would catch their attention? What terms or phrases would they be familiar with?

Subtitles: The Extra Information

A *subtitle* can be a useful tool to provide more context or information about your book. It can clarify the subject matter, specify the genre, or tease the content in more detail.

However, subtitles should be used prudently. An unnecessary or poorly chosen subtitle can clutter your book's title and make it less memorable. Consider using a subtitle if:

1. Your main title is ambiguous or metaphorical and you need to provide more clarity about the book's content.

2. Your book is part of a series and you want to denote its place in the series or its specific theme.

3. Your book is nonfiction, particularly in academic, self-help, or professional genres, where further

clarification or specificity can be helpful for potential readers.

In summary, the title of your book is an integral part of your book's identity. It's the first handshake with your reader, the calling card of your story, and the label that will stick when readers recommend your book to others. Don't rush the process. Take your time to consider your options, test them out, and choose the one that resonates the most with your book's content and your intended audience.

As you embark on your writing journey from within the walls of your current environment, remember that every aspect of your book, including the title, is a piece of you that you're sharing with the world. Your book could become a beacon of hope, a source of inspiration, or a thrilling escape for your readers. Make sure its title reflects that potential.

Choosing a title might seem like a small step in the vast project of writing and self-publishing a book. But as you are learning, each step is crucial in the journey of a thousand miles. So, take it seriously, give it thought, and choose a title that will unlock the door to your book's success. As an incarcerated author, you have unique experiences and perspectives to share. Let your title be the key that opens the minds of your readers to these unique insights.

Get Your Book Edited and Proofread

Before publishing your book, it's important, no, it's essential to get it *edited and proofread*. Listen up, no masterpiece has ever been created without a little polish and shine, feel me? In the gritty world of self-publishing, especially when you're doing it from the inside, your book has to stand out. Let's get it straight, your book is your voice, your story, your legacy. You can't afford to let it be drowned out by errors, grammatical mistakes, or lack of structure.

Now, editing and proofreading is no joke. They aren't the same thing, either. You need both. Yes, both. Editing is all about the big picture, it's looking at your plot, your character development, your pacing. It's about making sure your story flows right, keeps the reader engaged, and doesn't leave them scratching their heads wondering what just happened. It's about making sure your story is tight. Editing is the process of refining a work of writing. There are many types of edits, and there are many types of editors. The main types of editing are developmental editing, line editing, and copy editing:

1. **Developmental editing** – this is substantive editing, where you evaluate an entire manuscript for problems with plot structure, character arcs, overall story, consistency, etc. You might rearrange or delete chapters, condense, expand, or even rewrite the whole thing. Critiques should give you an idea of what to do for developmental edits.

2. **Line editing** – line editing is less about macro changes and more about micro changes. This is editing for things like style. It covers syntax, character dialect, realistic dialogue, verbiage, prose, etc.

3. **Copy editing (proof-reading)** – copy editing gets down to the tiny details, like proper sentence structure, consistent spelling, and grammar.

So, in short, developmental editing has a bigger impact on a longer piece, like a full novel. Line editing will clean up the language of a piece, but it won't change what actually happens in it, and Copy editing, or proof-reading, will check for technical mistakes.

It is helpful to note that there is a big difference between a self-edit and a professional edit.

Every book needs a *professional* edit!

Even if the writer is a professional editor themselves, editing their own book would require taking a several year gap between writing and editing to be able to come back to it with the new perspective required. You would effectively have to forget your entire book before you could do a proper job editing it, and even then, you'd have to have substantial editing experience to do it credibly. The short of it: hire an editor.

However, before the professional edit, is the self-edit. There are several rounds of self-editing a writer might partake in. When self-editing your book, it's important to pay attention to elements like grammar, spelling, and punctuation. You should also focus on refining your prose and ensuring that your story flows smoothly from beginning to end. You can also use *critique partners* and *beta readers* as tools in the editing process. Critiques aren't edits, but I'm mentioning them because I think they're such an important part of the writing process. You can get critiques from writing partners, beta readers, or hiring a professional. Critiques should point out problems with pacing, voice, character arcs, story structure, and other macro edits.

Proofreading (which some would consider the same as a Copy Edit), on the other hand, is all about the nitty-gritty. It's checking for typos, grammar mistakes, punctuation errors, and spelling mishaps. It's making sure your sentences make sense and that you're not confusing "there," "their," and "they're." It's the final polish that makes your book shine.

Now, you might be thinking, "I'm locked up. How do I get my book edited and proofread?" That's where your support network comes in. Reach out to friends or family on the outside who can help. If that's not an option, there are editing and proofreading services that can be accessed online. Even better, Prison Legal News (PLN) magazines are in heavy circulation throughout the prison system. There are typing services advertising on their pages or in their Classified Ads section all the time. Hit them up. Some of these services even offer special rates for incarcerated authors, so don't be shy about your situation. URBAN AINT DEAD even offers typing as one of the many services we provide for incarcerated aspiring authors who want to Self-Publishing their book, but simply want to hire us for a service. You can reach out to us via phone call or send us a letter and we'll be sure to get back with you:

URBAN AINT DEAD

P.O Box 448

Maybrook, NY 12543

(845) 636-3739

Remember, when you're self-publishing, especially from prison, you're not just competing with other incarcerated authors. You're up against every other author out there in the world. You need to make sure your book is the best it can be. So don't skip the editing and proofreading process. It's not just about fixing mistakes, it's about making your voice heard, loud and clear.

Design Your Book Cover

Designing your book cover is a crucial step in the self-publishing process. As the first point of contact with potential readers, your book cover should be visually appealing and convey a sense of professionalism. While designing a book cover can be challenging, especially without access to professional design software, there are various online tools and resources available to help you create a high-quality cover, even if you are currently incarcerated.

When creating your book cover, it's essential to consider the tone and themes of your book. For instance, if your book falls into the genre of urban fiction, you'll want to incorporate elements that reflect its bold and gritty nature. Urban imagery such as cityscapes, graffiti, or other elements that capture the essence of an urban environment can be effective in conveying the atmosphere and themes of your book.

To get started with designing your book cover, you can explore the following steps:

1. **Research and gather inspiration:** Look for book covers in the urban fiction genre or books with similar themes to yours. Examine their designs to understand what elements and styles resonate with you and your target audience.

2. **Choose appropriate colors:** Color plays a significant role in capturing the mood and grabbing readers' attention. In urban fiction, darker and more intense colors like deep blues, grays, or blacks can create a sense of intrigue and drama. However, it's important to ensure that the

colors you select harmonize well and are easily legible.

3. **Select fonts wisely:** Fonts contribute to the overall visual impact of your book cover. For urban fiction, consider using bold, edgy fonts that evoke a sense of urban energy. Experiment with different fonts to find the ones that align with your book's tone and genre, while still maintaining readability.

4. **Incorporate relevant imagery:** As mentioned earlier, urban imagery can be a powerful tool in reflecting the themes of your book. Consider using elements like cityscapes, silhouettes, graffiti, or other urban symbols that resonate with your story. However, ensure that the images you choose are of high quality and don't appear pixelated or blurry on the cover.

5. **Keep it simple and balanced:** While it's essential to make your cover visually striking, avoid overcrowding it with too many elements. Although I have seen it work, like with my 8th novel, *Murda Was The Case 3: Wrath Of A Boss,* a cluttered design might confuse or overwhelm potential readers. Strive for a balanced composition that draws the eye to the key elements while maintaining an overall sense of harmony.

6. **Test your design:** Once you have created your book cover, gather feedback from others, such as friends, fellow writers, or potential readers. Their insights can help you identify any areas that need improvement or provide valuable suggestions for enhancing the overall impact of your design.

Remember, your book cover should not only capture the essence of your story but also stand out among the numerous books available to readers. Investing time and effort into creating an eye-catching and professional book cover will significantly increase your chances of grabbing readers' attention and enticing them to explore your work further.

By following these steps and leveraging the available online tools, you can design a compelling book cover that reflects the themes of your book and piques the interest of potential readers, but if you or your outside assistant have no experience in this field, I strongly suggest you sub-contract a graphic designer to make one for you. Not just any graphic designer, either. Make sure they actually *design* book covers. You wouldn't hire someone who does mixtape cover to do your book cover. In my experience, it's not gonna come out right. I don't care how hard their mixtape covers are. It's gonna be a disaster for your book. Like anything, there are the exceptions. I know someone who does good covers, mixtapes, and designs covers for Tubi movies but even she isn't just all the way AI in my opinion. Decent, sometimes great, but I think she spreads herself too thin.

Cover design is also a Self-Publishing service that URBAN AINT DEAD offers. You can have your outside assistant book a service on our website: www.urbanaintdead .com

Click the *Book A Service* tab, and find *Covers*. We have some dope graphic designers on the team that can get you right with a market ready cover in any genre today. You can purchase it as an individual service or buy an Assistant Publishing Package (prices listed in the back). This way you can save money in the process.

Regardless of what, find you a designer who's locked in on books in whatever genre you wish to write in and in them you'll find a great cover artist. Be sure to have your people shop around as well. The prices are real competitive out there in them skreetz!

ISBN & Barcode Rundown

An *International Standard Book Number (ISBN)* is a unique identifier for books intended to be commercially available. It's a code which represents the specific title, author, edition, and format of a book.

Why is an ISBN necessary? It provides a standardized way for identifying books in the global marketplace. Libraries, bookstores, distributors, and online retailers use

ISBNs for ordering, listing, sales records, and inventory control. Without an ISBN, your book may be virtually invisible in the book industry.

Applying for an ISBN might require assistance from someone outside of prison. Here's how it's generally done:

1. **Bowker's MyIdentifiers Website (U.S.):** This is the official ISBN agency in the United States. Go to www.myidentifiers.com, create an account, and follow the instructions to purchase your ISBN. Remember that there are costs associated with obtaining an ISBN from Bowker.
2. **Library and Archives Canada (Canada):** For Canadian authors, ISBNs are free and can be obtained from Library and Archives Canada's website.
3. **Nielsen ISBN Store (U.K.):** For authors in the U.K., you can purchase ISBNs from the Nielsen ISBN Store.

The benefits of having an ISBN include:

1. **Standardized Identification:** The ISBN is a universally accepted system for book identification.
2. **Visibility:** With an ISBN, your book can be listed

on various online and offline platforms for sale or library cataloging.

3. **Sales Tracking:** ISBNs help in tracking sales and inventory.

4. **Legitimacy:** An ISBN adds a level of professionalism and legitimacy to your work.

Part II: The Barcode

A *barcode* is a machine-readable representation of data. In the context of books, the barcode typically encapsulates your ISBN, and often, the retail price information.

Why is a barcode necessary? It's primarily for retail and library systems. Barcodes allow for quick data entry and inventory management. When a book is sold in a bookstore or checked out in a library, the barcode is scanned, and the associated data is instantly brought up in the system.

Applying for a barcode also might require assistance from someone outside of prison. Here's how it's generally done:

1. **Bowker's MyIdentifiers Website (U.S.):** When you purchase an ISBN from Bowker, you can also choose to purchase a barcode.

2. **Online Barcode Generators:** There are also free online barcode generators, such as www.terryburton.co.uk/barcodewriter/generator.

However, ensure that the generated barcode is compatible with book industry standards.

The benefits of having a barcode include:

- **Efficient Inventory and Sales Management:** Barcodes allow for automated tracking, reducing the chance of human error.
- **Universally Understood:** Barcodes are universally accepted and can be read by scanners worldwide.
- **Price Information:** Barcodes can contain price information, making it easier for retailers.
- **Speed:** Scanning a barcode is much faster than manual data entry.

Both ISBNs and barcodes are crucial if you plan to make your book commercially available, especially in physical format. While the application process might be challenging from within prison, enlisting the aid of a trusted friend or family member on the outside could make it possible. Your book is an achievement and ensuring it has the right identifiers is an important step in its journey towards readers.

Part III: The Process from Behind Bars

Given your current situation, you may need to request assistance from a trusted person outside of the prison system to help you with obtaining an ISBN and barcode for your book. Let's break down the process:

Obtaining an ISBN

1. **Find a Helper:** This person will be responsible for navigating the ISBN acquisition process on your behalf. Make sure this person is reliable and understands the importance of the task.
2. **Choose the Right Agency:** Depending on the country of publication, your helper will need to approach the right agency. In the U.S., it is Bowker's MyIdentifiers Website; in Canada, it's Library and Archives Canada; and in the U.K., it's the Nielsen ISBN Store.
3. **Apply for ISBN:** Your helper will need to create an account with the chosen agency and follow the procedure to apply for an ISBN. This will involve providing some information about the book, such as the title, author name, and publisher.

Obtaining a Barcode

1. **Choose the Right Source:** If your helper obtained your ISBN from Bowker, they can also obtain a barcode there. Alternatively, they can use a free online barcode generator.

2. **Generate the Barcode:** Your helper will need to input the ISBN and, if applicable, the retail price of the book into the barcode generator. They should then save the barcode image in a format that can be incorporated into the book's cover design.

Remember, the clear and open communication with your helper is key in this process. They will need to understand the importance of each step and the details required.

Having an ISBN and barcode for your book, even while incarcerated, presents a unique opportunity. It allows your voice to be heard beyond the prison walls, making it possible for your work to reach bookstores, libraries, and readers' hands around the world. It's a crucial step in turning your manuscript into a book that can be widely distributed and recognized.

Typesetting Your Book

Typesetting is an often-overlooked but crucial step in the publishing process. It involves selecting and arranging type (fonts) in a way that makes your text readable and visually appealing. In the context of publishing your own book, it means arranging the text on the page so it's easy to read and consistent throughout the book.

How to Begin Typesetting

1. **Choosing a Font:** Look at different fonts and consider their readability and how they fit with the tone and style of your book. The most commonly used fonts for book bodies are Times New Roman, Garamond, and Georgia. These fonts are clear, easy to read, and work well in print.

2. **Layout:** Decide on the margins, line spacing, and paragraph indentation. This will largely depend on the size of your book. A typical book layout might have 1-inch margins, double line spacing, and a 0.5-inch paragraph indentation.

3. **Chapter Headings:** Decide how you want to handle chapter headings. They should be larger and possibly a different font than the body text to stand out.

4. **Page Numbers and Headers:** Decide where you want to place these and what they should contain.

Usually, page numbers go at the bottom center or top outer edges of the page, while headers go at the top and contain the book title, chapter title, or author name.

Practical Tips

- **Practicing Handwriting:** If you don't have access to a computer, you can still typeset your book by hand. Practice your handwriting to ensure it's as neat and consistent as possible. You can ask a friend or family member outside to help you choose a font and layout based on samples you create. You will still need your book typeset before going to print. The good thing is there are companies who except handwritten submissions; URBAN AINT DEAD is one of them.
- **Using a Typewriter:** Some prisons allow the use of typewriters. If you have access to one, you can use it to create a clean, consistent text.
- **Proofreading:** Always proofread your work, or have someone else proofread it for you, to ensure there are no mistakes or inconsistencies in the typesetting.

- **Getting Help:** If someone outside can assist, you can write your book by hand, have it transcribed and typeset professionally, and then sent back to you for review.

Pros and Cons of Skipping Typesetting
Pros

1. **Time-Saving:** You can save a significant amount of time by skipping this step, allowing you to focus on writing and editing.

Cons

1. **Readability:** A poor typeset book can be difficult to read and off-putting to potential readers. Good typesetting enhances readability and the overall aesthetic of the book.
2. **Professionalism:** Books that are not properly typeset can appear amateurish, which might deter potential readers.
3. **Consistency:** Typesetting ensures consistency in the typography throughout your book. Inconsistencies can distract readers and look unprofessional.

Remember, the goal of typesetting is to make your book as readable and attractive as possible. Even if you're working under constraints, there are ways to ensure your book is well typeset and ready for publication.

Pricing Your Ebook

Pricing your ebook requires your careful attention. Setting the right price can significantly impact your ebook's accessibility, profitability, and success in the marketplace. For incarcerated authors, understanding the nuances of Kindle Direct Publishing (KDP) and Kindle Unlimited (KU) is essential, as these platforms offer unique opportunities and constraints.

Kindle Direct Publishing (KDP) Overview

KDP is Amazon's self-publishing platform that allows you to publish both ebooks and paperbacks for free. It's a popular choice among self-published authors due to its wide reach and the autonomy it provides.

Pricing on KDP

When pricing your ebook on KDP, consider the following:

1. **Royalty Options:**

A. 70% Royalty: For ebooks priced between $2.99 and $9.99, you're eligible to earn 70% of the list price minus delivery costs. This option is available in select countries.

B. 35% Royalty: If your book is priced outside the range above or if the 70% royalty option isn't available in your country, you'll receive 35% of the list price.

2. Delivery Costs: These are subtracted from your royalties and are based on the file size of your ebook. Larger files with lots of images will incur higher costs.

3. KDP Select: Enrolling your ebook in KDP Select gives you additional promotional tools, including the ability to offer your book for free for a limited time or as part of a countdown deal. However, it requires exclusivity to Amazon for at least 90 days. For this reason, I don't publish ebooks outside of Amazon.

Kindle Unlimited (KU) and How It Affects Pricing

Kindle Unlimited is a subscription service that allows readers to read as many books as they want for a monthly fee. When you enroll your ebook in KDP Select, it automatically becomes part of KU.

Kindle Unlimited is so widely used amongst readers you would be missing out on so much exposure by not having your books available on there at all times. This is how most authors are making their money these days. It's free for the readers, but authors are paid by the page reads. We know how much people love free stuff.

You see where I'm going with this?

Earnings Through KU

1. Like I said, authors are paid based on the number of pages read by KU subscribers. The fund from which authors are paid is determined by Amazon and varies each month.
2. You'll still retain your royalties from direct sales alongside KU earnings.

Considerations for Incarcerated Authors

As an aspiring author in prison, you will face unique challenges when publishing and pricing your ebook. Here are some key points to keep in mind:

1. **Outside Assistance:** You may need a trusted friend, family member, or professional to manage

your KDP account. You will require email access and the ability to manage digital documents, which may not be feasible from within prison.

2. **Communication:** Establish clear and consistent communication with your proxy to ensure they understand your pricing strategy and any promotional campaigns you wish to run.

3. **Access to Information:** Keeping informed about the performance of your ebook and any changes to KDP or KU policies can be challenging. Your proxy should provide regular updates and assist with any necessary adjustments to your pricing or marketing strategy.

4. **Legal Considerations:** It's important to understand that any income earned from your ebook sales may affect your prison account, and you may need to report this income for tax purposes. Ensure that you or your proxy are aware of the legal implications.

5. **Document Accessibility:** You will need to have your manuscript in a digital format that complies with KDP's submission requirements. This may involve dictating your work to someone on the outside who can format and upload it for you.

6. **Pricing Strategy:** With limited access to market data, you'll have to rely on your outside contact to research comparable titles and help you set a

competitive price. Monitor your book's performance and adjust your pricing strategy accordingly.

When pricing your ebook, consider the value it offers to readers, the pricing of similar books in your genre, and the goals you have for your book. A well-thought-out pricing strategy can enhance your book's visibility, attract more readers, and maximize your earnings, all of which contribute to your success as a self-published author from prison.

Optimizing Your Earnings with KDP Select and Kindle Unlimited

When enrolled in KDP Select, your ebook's presence in Kindle Unlimited can be a double-edged sword. On one hand, it increases your book's exposure to a dedicated reader base who are voracious readers, but on the other, your earnings are dependent on the number of pages read. Here's how to navigate this:

1. **Page Reads:** Focus on writing compelling content that keeps readers engaged. The more pages KU subscribers read, the more you earn. Serialized content or books with cliffhangers may encourage readers to continue reading your series.

2. **Book Length:** Longer books may potentially earn more through KU, as earnings are based on page reads. However, quality should never be sacrificed for quantity—readers are looking for engaging, well-written content.

3. **Promotions:** Utilize the promotional tools offered by KDP Select to increase visibility. Free book promotions can drive up your book's ranking, leading to increased visibility once the promotion ends.

Setting the Right Price

The price of your ebook should reflect its value while also taking into account the competitive landscape. Here's what to consider:

1. **Genre Standards:** Different genres often have standard pricing tiers. Research the pricing of top-selling ebooks in your genre to find a competitive price point.

2. **Pricing Flexibility:** Don't be afraid to experiment with pricing. You can adjust the price based on sales performance, special promotions, or to react to market changes.

3. **International Markets:** KDP allows you to set prices for different international markets. This can be critical if you have content that may appeal to readers in specific countries.

Understanding KDP's Pricing Support

KDP offers a pricing support feature that suggests a price based on maximizing earnings. However, as you may not have direct access to this feature, instruct your proxy to explore these suggestions and use them as a guideline, adjusting as necessary to fit your specific strategy.

Communicating with Your Proxy

As you rely on an intermediary to handle the intricacies of publishing on KDP and KU, it is imperative that you establish a robust and trusting relationship. Your success hinges on the ability of your proxy to act on your behalf. Discuss your vision, objectives, and pricing strategy in detail with them.

Legal and Financial Consideration

1. **Inmate Trust Accounts:** Income from book sales will typically be reported by Amazon and may be subject to garnishment or fees depending on the regulations of the correctional facility.

2. **Taxes:** Your proxy should help manage the financial aspects, including taxes owed on your royalties. You may need to file tax returns to remain compliant with IRS regulations. Unless you plan to run it up for the Feds to come take it away. You can stay in the streets and do that, though. Play it smart. This is your legitimate exit.

3. **Contracts and Rights:** Ensure that any agreement with your proxy is clearly documented, especially concerning rights and royalties. You may want to consult with a legal professional to protect your interests.

Conclusion

Setting the price of your ebook is a strategic decision that can have a significant impact on your book's success. As an incarcerated author, while you may face unique challenges, with the right support network and a clear understanding of Kindle Direct Publishing and Kindle Unlimited, you can successfully navigate the self-publishing landscape. Remember to stay informed, adaptable, and proactive in your approach, even from within the prison system, to maximize the potential of your ebook.

Personally, and you may not like the sound of this, I would price my ebook for $0.99¢. Especially if it's the first of a series. It's difficult to get readers to try new authors as it is. Price it at $0.99¢ and up it as you go up in the series. For example:

·Book 1 - $0.99¢

·Book 2 – $2.99

·Book 3 - $4.99

And so on, and so on...you don't want that number to get too high, though. It's still an ebook after all. So, depending on how many parts are in your series, you may want to go back and adjust the prices.

My point was, once you have the readers hooked, you can charge them as you please. All the same, for business sake, be reasonable. To do that, you have to research your market within your genre. See what your competitors are doing because different genres have different prices. Mainly because the target audience is different. James Patterson's audience may be willing to spend more on a book than David Weaver's, just as Taylor Swift's fans may be willing to spend more on an album than Lil Boosie's fans. Figure out what works for you and build from there.

<u>Audiobook</u>

In the landscape of self-publishing, the realm of audio-books has grown exponentially and presents a unique opportunity for authors, including those who are incarcerated. Two prominent platforms in the audiobook industry are Audible's Audiobook Creation Exchange (ACX) and Podium Publishing. Both platforms offer distinct pathways for getting your book into the ears of listeners, but each has its own set of steps, requirements, and considerations, which we will explore in this section.

Audible's Audiobook Creation Exchange (ACX)

ACX is a marketplace where authors, narrators, and producers come together to create audiobooks. It's the leading platform for audiobook production and distribution, with the largest market share, being a subsidiary of Amazon. Here's how it works:

1. **Rights and Eligibility:** First, you must have the audio rights to your book. If you self-published your book on platforms like Amazon's Kindle Direct Publishing (KDP), you likely retained these rights. However, if you are incarcerated, you may need to work through a trusted contact outside of prison to manage the online aspects of the process. Have them create you an account on ACX. Doing so will require personal identification information and tax details. Make sure it's someone you trust.

2. **Creating an Account:** Normally, you would create an

account on ACX and claim your book by searching for it on the platform. Given your circumstance, your outside contact would need to do this on your behalf. After signing up, they'll create a profile, and then they can post your titles to ACX. This involves describing your book and specifying what you are looking for in a narrator (also called a Producer).

3. **Production:** Once your book is claimed, you can either produce the audiobook yourself or find a producer/narrator. You can post a script and invite narrators to audition or search through narrator profiles and make offers. For those in prison, this step requires a collaborator who can handle the production process, as you won't have the means to record high-quality audio or directly engage with narrators. Once you've selected a narrator, you'll enter into an agreement with them. The production process then begins, with the narrator recording and producing the audiobook.

4. **Agreement:** You'll need to agree on the payment terms with the producer/narrator, which can be a pay-per-finished-hour rate or a royalty share agreement where the narrator gets a portion of the sales.

5. **Production and Approval:** The producer will record and edit the audiobook. You or your designated contact will have the chance to review the audio and request changes before approving the final product.

6. **Distribution:** After approval, ACX will distribute the audiobook to Audible, Amazon, and iTunes. You'll earn

royalties based on sales, the rate of which depends on the distribution option chosen.

Podium Publishing

Podium Publishing is known for its success with indie authors and its focus on science fiction and fantasy genres. Unlike ACX, Podium is a traditional audiobook publisher, which means they select and acquire audiobooks to produce, rather than creating an open market for production.

1. **Submission:** Authors can submit their work directly to Podium for consideration, but due to the nature of your circumstances, you would need someone on the outside to manage this process.

2. **Selection Process:** Podium reviews submissions and selects books they believe will succeed in the audiobook format. They look for well-reviewed books with a strong sales track record.

3. **Production:** If selected, Podium will handle all aspects of production, from narration to editing and mastering the audiobook.

4. **Royalties:** Authors receive royalty payments, the specifics of which are outlined in the contract offered by Podium. This contract should be reviewed by a lawyer or trusted advisor.

. . .

What You Can and Can't Do

As a self-publishing incarcerated author there are several limitations to consider:

A. Direct Access: You cannot directly access online platforms, record audio, or communicate with narrators and producers. You need an intermediary.

B. Legal and Contractual Matters: Any contracts or agreements will need to be reviewed and signed by someone on your behalf outside of prison.

C. Quality Control: You will rely on your outside contact to ensure the audiobook's quality meets the industry standard.

D. Marketing: While ACX and Podium will distribute your audiobook, marketing efforts to promote the book will need to be conducted by someone outside prison walls.

Best Practices

A. Find a Trustworthy Contact: An agent, friend, family member, or lawyer who can act on your behalf is crucial.

B. Communicate Clearly: Provide detailed instructions and feedback through your contact to ensure your vision for the audiobook is realized.

C. Understand Your Rights: Know what rights you are granting to a publisher or distributor and what you retain.

D. Stay Informed: Keep up-to-date with correspondence from your contact, publishers, and any legal advisors.

E. Be Patient: The audiobook production process can be lengthy, and being incarcerated adds another layer of complexity.

Conclusion

In summary, while the process of creating an audiobook from prison is challenging, it's most definitely possible. With the right outside assistance, an understanding of the platforms available, and diligent management of your book's production and distribution, your story can reach an audience in the ever-expanding world of audiobooks.

Choosing and Uploading Your Book To A Distribution Platform

When it comes to self-publishing, ***choosing the right platform to distribute your book*** is crucial. While it may seem daunting at first, understanding the pros and cons of each platform can help you make an informed decision. Here are some of the top platforms for self-publishing and their respective pros and cons:

I. Book Baby.

Pros:

A. **Comprehensive package:** Book Baby offers a one-stop-shop solution that covers everything from book formatting, cover design, distribution, and even promotion.

B. **Wide distribution:** Your book will be available on all major online retailers, including Amazon, Barnes & Noble, and Apple's iBookstore.

C. **Print on demand:** Unlike traditional publishing, you don't have to worry about printing a large number of books upfront.

Cons:

A. **High upfront cost:** Compared to other platforms, Book Baby can be more expensive initially.

B. **Outside assistance required:** Due to the restrictions on internet access in many prisons, you will need someone outside to help you with the publishing process.

2. Kindle Direct Publishing (KDP).

Pros:

A. **Easy to use:** KDP's interface is user-friendly, making it easy to publish your book.

B. **High royalties:** You can earn up to 70% in royalties from sales in certain countries.

C. **KDP Select:** This program gives you the opportunity to earn more money through Kindle Unlimited and Kindle Owners' Lending Library.

Cons:

A. **Limited distribution:** Your book is only sold on Amazon platforms.

B. **Outside assistance required:** As with Book Baby, you'll need someone on the outside to assist with uploading and managing your book due to internet restrictions in prison.

3. Lulu.

Pros:

A. **Print and eBook options:** Lulu offers both print-on-demand and eBook distribution.

B. **Global distribution:** Your book will be available on Amazon, Barnes & Noble, and other bookstores and libraries worldwide.

Cons:

A. **Extra fees for services:** While it's free to publish, extra services like editing and book cover design come with a cost.

B. **Outside assistance needed:** Internet restrictions mean you'll need outside help to upload and manage your book.

4. IngramSpark.

Pros:

A. **Wide distribution:** IngramSpark has an extensive

distribution network, making your book available worldwide.

B. **Print and eBook options:** Like Lulu, it offers both print-on-demand and eBook distribution.

C. **Upload:** As of early 2023, it's officially free to upload your books. That's right, they've waved their setup cost. My guess is that it's an attempt to level the playing field with Amazon, but what do I know? I'm in a cell with you. Whatever the reason, it's good news for us.

Cons:

A. **Not user friendly.** May be a little difficult to navigate. That's me being mild. This platform is a real headache to use.

B. **Templates:** Certain templates may identify to their system as low quality and will red flag your project as an image distortion. Be careful with that. You may want to keep the interior design simple if you're going this route.

C. **Outside help required:** You'll need someone to assist you with the publishing process.

5. Draft2Digital.

Pros:

A. **Easy to use:** The platform is user-friendly with a straightforward publishing process.

B. **Wide distribution:** Draft2Digital distributes your book to a variety of online retailers.

Cons:

A. **No Amazon distribution:** If you want to sell on Amazon, you'll have to do it yourself via KDP.

B. **Outside help needed:** As with the other platforms, you'll need outside help due to internet restrictions.

6. Blurb.

Pros:

A. **Unique formats:** Blurb allows for the creation of photo books, magazines, and other unique formats, in addition to traditional book types.

B. **Creative control:** You have a lot of freedom in terms of design and layout.

Cons:

A. **Limited distribution:** While your book can be sold on Amazon and the Blurb Bookstore, distribution is not as extensive as some other platforms.

B. **Outside help required:** As with the other platforms, you'll need assistance from someone on the outside to handle the publishing process.

. . .

Before choosing a platform, it's crucial to consider the kind of book you've written, your budget, and your specific needs as an author. Once you've made a decision, you can work with someone on the outside to handle the uploading and management process. This can be a trusted friend, family member, or even a professional service, as long as they understand your vision and can accurately represent your interests.

Remember to provide this person with all the necessary materials and information, including the final manuscript, any illustrations or diagrams, and a clear outline of how you'd like the book to be presented. *Communication* is key in ensuring your book is published just the way you envisioned it.

Also, be mindful that while self-publishing allows you to retain control and rights over your book, it also means you're responsible for its marketing and promotion. Consider this in your planning and ensure you have a strategy to get your book noticed once it's published.

Self-publishing can be a rewarding journey, even from within the confines of prison. With careful planning, patience, and perseverance, you can successfully share your work with the world.

"Build your tribe, build your own customer base, know your audience," author Paris Iman says. *"THEY are your support. Be*

confident in your work. Be head strong, be resilient and stay focused."

For deeper insight into the world of Self-Publishing, purchase her book, *Self-Publishing Guide To Success: Step-By-Step Guide To Becoming A Saavy Self-Publisher.*

Also, have your outside assistant visit our website www.urbanaintdead.com, and click on the "Book A Service" tab where we offer different self-publishing services for authors who want to do their own thing, but simply want to hire us as a sub-contractor for specific tasks that they have no resource for. We offer covers, typing, editing, and publishing consultations.

CHAPTER 7

Dealing with Legal Issues

Legal issues in publishing are not just obstacles; they're opportunities to define and defend the value of your work." – Offers a positive perspective on the role of legal considerations.

By now, you should realize that publishing a book from prison can be a challenging and complex process, but particularly even more so when it comes to navigating legal issues, such as censorship or copyright infringement. As an author, it's important to understand the legal considerations involved in publishing your work, in order to avoid potential legal problems and protect your rights as a writer. In this chapter, we will explore the *legal issues* that authors may encounter when publishing from prison, including copyright law, libel and defamation, and First Amendment rights. I will also provide practical advice and resources for managing these issues in a way that is both effective and legally sound.

Copyright Law

Copyright law is a critical consideration for any author, particularly when it comes to self-publishing. Under U.S. copyright law, the creator of an original work automatically owns the copyright to that work, including the right to reproduce, distribute, and display the work.

As an author publishing from prison, it's important to ensure that you own the copyright to your work, and that you have the legal right to publish it. In my own opinion, this should be done before even submitting your manuscript. No, it doesn't have to be, and some reputable publishers will secure the copyright in your name on your behalf (the way they should), but people don't always play fair with incarcerated people. On top of that, them being free gives them more leverage than you to put copyright in their name and put it out first. Protect yourself.

Owning the copyright to your work and having the legal right to publish it may require obtaining permission from any co-authors or contributors, as well as ensuring that any copyrighted material included in your work (such as song lyrics or quotes from other authors) is properly attributed and used with permission; that is assuming there are any. If not, nothing to worry about on that end.

In addition, it's important to consider the role of copyright law in protecting your work from piracy and unauthorized distribution. This may involve registering your copyright with the U.S. Copyright Office or using digital rights management tools to prevent unauthorized copying or distribution of your work.

For free information on copyright law to get an even more in-depth understanding, have someone visit www.copyright.gov or write the address below, sending a self-addressed stamped envelope:

Library of Congress (Copyright Office)
101 Independence Ave. S.E.
Washington, D.C. 20559-6000

Libel and Defamation

Another legal issue that authors may encounter is the risk of **libel and defamation.** *Libel* refers to the publication of false or harmful statements that damage a person's reputation, while *defamation* refers to similar statements made orally or through other forms of communication.

As an author, it's important to be mindful of the potential for libel and defamation in your work, particularly if your writing is based on real people or events. This may require taking steps to ensure that your work is based on accurate information and avoiding making statements that could be construed as defamatory.

In addition, it's important to understand the legal defenses that may be available in the event of a libel or defamation claim. These defenses may include truth, privilege, and fair comment, and can help protect you from legal liability in the event of a lawsuit.

First Amendment Rights

Finally, as an author, it's important to understand your *First Amendment rights* to free speech and expression:

"Congress shall make no law respecting an establishment of religion or prohibiting the free exercise thereof; ***or abridging the freedom of speech,*** *or of the press; or the right of the people peaceably to assemble, and to petition the Government for a redress of grievances."*

The First Amendment protects your right to publish your work and express your ideas, even if those ideas are controversial or unpopular. The good thing is that even as a prisoner, you *still* have that **right!!**

However, it's important to understand that First Amendment rights are not absolute and may be limited in certain circumstances. For example, the government may impose restrictions on speech that is deemed to be obscene or incites violence or may require permits or licenses for certain types of public expression.

In addition, private individuals and organizations may have legal rights to protect their reputations and privacy, which can limit your ability to publish certain types of information. It's important to be mindful of these limitations and to seek legal advice if you are unsure about the legality of your work. For the most part, though, fiction authors don't have these issues. It's more of a non-fiction thing, but something I want you to be mindful of all the same. You never know. Some people like to go after authors whose fiction is loosely based around true events.

A lot of you purchased this book for different reasons. Some of it may be for you, and some of it may not be. I wanted to cover a wide range of topics involved when publishing from prison, so some of the information provided you may not have been looking for but found or may find out it was needed. Take heed to everything mentioned.

It's important to understand the legal issues involved in order to protect your rights as a writer and avoid potential legal problems. By taking steps to ensure that you own the copyrights to your work, you can avoid any unnecessary drama. You see, *owning* your intellectual property is key in this game; it's your golden ticket, your pass to the big leagues. Nobody can take that from you without your permission. So, make sure you get your copyrights in order and save yourself from folks who might want to snatch your ideas.

Now, back to the matter of the First Amendment. You might be in the chain-gang, but you still got rights. But remember, when you're weaving your tales, you can't tarnish the reputation of real people or invade their privacy. You have to be careful with that, even if you're writing fiction. If folks think you're talking about them, they may come after you claiming defamation or invasion of privacy and ignoring that "based on a true story" disclaimer you put at the front.

So, how do you sidestep this? Easy. You mix things up. Change names, locations, physical appearances, anything that could link your character to a real person. Keep it all *fictional*. If you're unsure, consult with a legal professional. They can help you navigate these waters.

Lastly, remember, you're an artist, so don't let these legal issues stifle your creativity. Yes, there are rules, but within these rules, there's plenty of room to create, express, and tell your story.

Publishing a book from prison ain't no walk in the park, but it's a journey worth taking. It's about leaving a legacy, sharing your truth, and reaching people who need to hear your story. It's your voice, your power, and you can never let anyone take that from you.

So, don't just read this book, *use it*. *Learn* from it. Let it *guide* you, because in this challenging journey, knowledge is your best weapon. It's your blueprint to navigate the legal maze of publishing. And always remember, your voice matters. Your story matters. Write like you mean it, and let the world hear your roar.

In the end, this ain't just about publishing a book, it's about fighting for your right to be heard, no matter where you are. That's the real power of the First Amendment. So, take that power, claim it, and let it fuel your journey from a prisoner to a published author.

Dealing With Legal Issues 2: Son Of Sam Laws

The Son of Sam laws are a series of laws passed by various states in the United States to prevent criminals from profiting from their crimes. I first caught wind of them (as I'm sure some of you did also) on a publishing flyer that was circulating by *Midnight Express*. At the time, I was ignorant to these laws and had no idea they existed. They were passed almost forty years before the time I came across them and are almost fifty years old now. These laws are named after David Berkowitz, who was known as the "Son of Sam" and received large sums of money for writing about his crimes.

In this section, I will explore the origins of the Son of Sam laws, their purpose, and their relevance in 2023. As an incarcerated author, I will provide an in-depth analysis of the Son of Sam laws and their impact on society.

Origins of the Son of Sam Laws

The Son of Sam laws were first passed in New York in 1977, in response to David Berkowitz's attempts to profit from his crimes. Berkowitz, who was convicted of a series of murders in the mid-1970s, wrote a book about his crimes and attempted to sell the rights to the story for a large sum of money.

This sparked outrage among the public and lawmakers, who were concerned that criminals would be able to profit from their crimes and use the money to fund their legal defenses or to continue engaging in criminal activity. In response, New York passed the first Son of Sam law, which required that any profits earned from the sale of a criminal's story be placed in an escrow account for the benefit of the victims.

Other states soon followed suit, passing their own versions of the Son of Sam laws. Today, the laws vary by state, but all are designed to prevent criminals from profiting from their crimes.

Purpose of the Son of Sam Laws

The primary *purpose of the Son of Sam laws* is to prevent criminals from profiting from their crimes. This serves several important purposes.

First, it ensures that criminals are not able to use the proceeds from their crimes to fund their legal defenses or to continue engaging in criminal activity. This is particularly important in cases where the criminal may have a large following or fan base, as the profits from their story or merchandise could be significant.

Second, the Son of Sam laws help to protect the victims of the crime by ensuring that any profits earned from the sale of the criminal's story are used to compensate the victims or their families. This provides a measure of justice and closure for the victims, who may have suffered greatly as a result of the crime.

Who the Son of Sam Laws Affect

The Son of Sam laws primarily affect criminals who have committed high-profile crimes and may have a following or fan base. This includes serial killers, mass shooters, and other notorious criminals who may be the subject of media attention.

However, the laws can also affect individuals who are not necessarily criminals, but who have been accused of crimes or who have been the subject of media attention as a result of their association with a crime. For example, a person who is acquitted of a crime but who still receives media attention may be subject to the Son of Sam laws if they attempt to profit from their story.

Relevance of the Son of Sam Laws in 2023

The relevance of the Son of Sam laws in 2023 is a matter of debate. Some argue that the laws are outdated and unnecessary, as advances in technology have made it easier than ever for criminals to profit from their crimes without the need for a book or movie deal.

Others argue that the laws are still relevant and necessary, particularly in cases where a criminal may have a large following or fan base. In addition, the laws serve an important role in providing some sense of justice for victims and their families. These laws ensure that criminals can't just cash in on their notorious acts and live in luxury, while the people they hurt are left to pick up the pieces. It's about balance and keeping the scales from tipping in favor of those who broke the rules.

In 2023, with the rise of social media and online platforms, the Son of Sam laws are more relevant than ever. The digital era, with its vlogs, podcasts, and self-published e-books, has opened up a whole new world for storytelling. It ain't just about traditional book or movie deals no more. A criminal with a smart phone and a Wi-Fi connection could potentially make big bucks off their crimes just by sharing their side of the story online. The Son of Sam laws haven't yet adapted to this evolving landscape, but to ensure that no profit from criminal notoriety slips through the cracks, they may.

On the flip side, some argue that these laws infringe on First Amendment rights. They say that even a criminal has a right to tell their story, to express themselves, and that prof-iting from their story is just a side effect. But let's keep it real, the issue ain't about silencing anyone. It's about making sure that crime doesn't pay, *literally*. It's about ensuring that justice is served, not just in the courtroom but in the market-place, too.

In the context of publishing a book from prison, these laws are a crucial consideration. If you're writing about your experiences within the confines of the law, that's one thing. But if you're planning to profit from the details of your crimes, you best believe the Son of Sam laws will come into play. So, stay informed, be smart about it, and remember, justice ain't just about what happens in the courtroom, it's about what happens out here in the real world, too.

Marketing Your Book

Marketing is crucial to the success of your book, and it's important to have a plan in place to promote your work. The first book I released did alright the first month, but those sales were from the support of my family and friends. The next month sales were lighter and continued to dwindle with each passing month. It wasn't long before I realized that writing the book and putting it out was only half the battle. I had to get active in marketing my book, but how?

In this chapter, we'll explore the different marketing strategies you can use to get your book in the hands of readers, with and without the help of an outside assistant.

Marketing your book from prison can be difficult, but it is

essential if you want to gain readership and generate income. The key to successfully marketing your book is to understand your target audience and create a marketing plan that speaks directly to them. With the right strategies and a bit of creativity, you can successfully promote your book and reach your target audience. This chapter will provide an overview of the marketing process and introduce some of the key concepts that you will need to consider when promoting your book.

Identifying Your Target Audience

The first step in marketing your book, whether you're doing it from the slammer to the penthouse, is to know who you're talking to. You have to know who's going to vibe with your story, who's going to crack open that cover and not want to put it down. That's your target audience. Your *target audience* is the group of people who are most likely to be interested in your book. This group can be defined by factors such as age, gender, location, interests, and reading habits. Your target audience isn't just some random group of people out there. No, these are the people who are going to connect with your words, with your struggle, with your triumph. It's your job to figure out what they're into and even how they like to read. Some people like a hardcover in their hands, while others are all about that e-book life.

To identify your target audience, start by thinking about

the themes and subject matter of your book; like, really dig into it. What's it about? Who's gonna feel that? Who is most likely to be interested in these topics? For example, if your book is about the struggles of growing up in an inner-city neighborhood, your target audience may be young adults who have experienced similar challenges. If your books is about cooking, your target audience may primarily be women between the ages of 18 to 35. Or, if you're book is about how to publish from prison, your audience may be incarcerated men and women between the ages of 21 through 45.

Once you have identified your target audience, you can begin to develop a marketing plan that speaks directly to them. That's right, it's time to make some moves. You have to get your book where they can see it, where they can touch it. This may involve creating targeted ads on social media platforms, getting your book in a catalog that they have access to, placing an Ad in a magazine in which they have a subscription, and partnering with local organizations that serve your target audience. Partner with them, and you're halfway there. And let's not forget about book clubs and reading groups. These people are always looking for the next big thing to read, and if you can get your book in their hands, you've got a whole crew spreading the word about your work.

That's how you identify your target audience. Know them, understand them, and reach them where they're at.

This isn't just about selling a book; it's about sharing your story with the people who need to hear it. And that's no cap.

Developing a Marketing Plan

Once you have identified your target audience, it is time to develop a marketing plan. A marketing plan is a roadmap that outlines the steps you will take to promote your book and reach your target audience. Your marketing plan should include the following elements:

1. **Goals:** What do you hope to achieve through your marketing efforts? Are you looking to increase sales, build your brand, or generate buzz?
2. **Budget:** How much money do you have to spend on marketing? This will determine the types of marketing activities that you can pursue.
3. **Channels:** What channels will you use to reach your target audience? This may include social media, email marketing, advertising, and public relations.
4. **Tactics:** What specific tactics will you use to reach your target audience? This may include running ads on social media, hosting book signings and readings, and reaching out to book reviewers, bloggers, and bookstagrammers.

. . .

Marketing Your Book Without an Outside Assistant

Congratulations on completing your manuscript! Now that you have your book in hand, it's time to embark on the exciting journey of marketing it to the world. While being incarcerated presents unique challenges, it doesn't mean you can't effectively promote your book. In this section, we will explore various methods for marketing your book without relying on an outside assistant. Remember, persistence and creativity are key to achieving success!

1. Leverage Prison Resources.

Utilize the resources available within the prison system to spread the word about your book. Here are a few strategies to consider:

A. Word of Mouth: Share your story and passion for writing with fellow inmates, correctional officers, and prison staff. Encourage them to spread the word to their friends and family on the outside.

B. Prison Library: Approach the prison library staff and request them to carry copies of your book. This will make it accessible to other inmates who may be interested in reading it.

. . .

2. Develop a Strong Online Presence.

Even from behind bars, you can establish an online presence to promote your book. Here's how

A. Author Website: Create a simple website dedicated to your writing and book. Include an author bio, book synopsis, and ordering instructions. You can use platforms like WordPress or Blogger, which offer free website creation tools.

B. Social Media: While direct access to the internet may not be possible, you can write letters to friends or family members requesting them to create social media profiles on your behalf. They can share updates, book excerpts, and engage with potential readers.

3. Utilize Traditional Media Channels.

Explore avenues within the traditional media landscape to get your book noticed:

A. Local Newspapers: Write a well-crafted press release about your book and send it to local newspapers. Highlight your unique circumstances and the journey that led you to write the book. This human-interest angle may pique their interest.

B. Radio Shows: Research radio stations that focus on book reviews or author interviews. Write a compelling letter or email to these stations, explaining your situation and requesting an opportunity to talk about your book.

. . .

4. Engage with Book Clubs and Writing Communities.

Connect with book clubs and writing communities to expand your network and gain exposure:

A. Correspondence Courses: Many prisons offer correspondence courses for inmates. Enroll in a creative writing course to enhance your skills and connect with other aspiring writers who may be interested in reading your book.

B. Pen Pal Networks: Reach out to pen pal networks that connect inmates with people on the outside. Share your story and offer to send a signed copy of your book to interested individuals. This can generate word-of-mouth promotion and potentially lead to positive reviews.

5. Write Articles and Guest Blog Posts.

Sharpen your writing skills further by contributing articles or guest blog posts related to your book's themes. Look for websites, magazines, or blogs that cover topics similar to those explored in your book. Craft engaging, well-researched pieces that captivate readers and mention your book at the end.

6. Seek Local Speaking Engagements.

If you have the opportunity to participate in prison

programs or events, make the most of it:

A. Inmate Programs: Many prisons organize programs where inmates share their experiences and insights. Participate in these events and bring copies of your book to sell or give away.

B. Community Outreach: If your prison allows community outreach programs, volunteer to speak at local schools, libraries, or community centers. Prepare a captivating presentation about your journey as an incarcerated author and offer signed copies of your book for sale. This can help raise awareness and generate interest in your work.

7. Participate in Writing Contests.

A. Look for writing contests that accept submissions from incarcerated individuals. Winning or being recognized in a contest can provide valuable exposure for your book. Research the guidelines and submission requirements carefully, and ensure your manuscript meets the specified criteria.

8. Collaborate with Prison Publications.

A. If your facility has a prison newspaper or literary magazine, submit excerpts or articles related to your book. This can help you reach a captive audience and generate curiosity among fellow inmates.

. . .

9. Utilize Direct Mail Marketing.

While you may not have access to the internet or email, you can still engage in direct mail marketing:

A. Book Reviewers: Research book reviewers who accept physical copies of books for review. Write personalized letters to these reviewers, introducing yourself and your book, and request their consideration for a review.

B. Independent Bookstores: Reach out to independent bookstores that support local authors. Send them a copy of your book along with a professional letter explaining your circumstances and requesting that they carry your book on their shelves.

10. Develop a Brand Identity.

Create a unique brand identity for yourself as an author, even from behind bars:

A. Author Signature: Sign your letters, correspondence, and promotional materials with a distinctive signature that represents your brand. This adds a personal touch and helps readers remember you.

B. Author Business Cards: Design and print business cards with your author name, book title, contact information (e.g., a trusted friend's address), and a brief description of your book. Distribute these cards to individuals you correspond with or during speaking engagements.

C. Leverage: Remember, marketing your book without an outside assistant requires determination and resourcefulness. Leverage the resources available to you, both within the prison system and through indirect channels. Be proactive, engage with potential readers, and share your unique story. While the road may be challenging, your creativity and perseverance can help you reach an audience and make your mark as an incarcerated author.

Marketing Your Book With an Outside Assistant

Alright, so you've put pen to paper, poured your soul into each page, and now you've got a book on your hands. But what's next? You might be behind bars, but that doesn't mean your story has to be. With the help of an outside assistant, you can get your book in the hands of readers who need to hear your voice. Here's how you do it, step by step:

1. **Develop Your Brand:** First things first, you gotta know who you are as an author and what your book stands for. This is your brand. Your assistant can help you narrow down your unique selling points, and make sure everything from your book cover to your social media bios reflects this brand.

2. **Website Creation:** Your assistant can set up an author website for you. This is your digital home,

a place where readers can learn more about you and your book. It should have a bio, a synopsis of your book, and a way for readers to get in touch or sign up for updates.

3. **Social Media Presence:** Social media is where you connect with your readers. Your assistant can maintain your accounts, post updates, and interact with followers. Just make sure they're sharing authentic content that reflects your voice and your brand.

4. **Email Marketing:** Your assistant can manage an email list for you. This is a direct line to your readers' inboxes, where you can share updates, sneak peeks, and special offers.

5. **Book Trailer:** A video trailer for your book is like a movie trailer, but for your book. Your assistant can help create one that captures the essence of your story and share it on your website and social media accounts.

6. **Press Releases:** Your assistant can write and send press releases about your book to news outlets, blogs, and other platforms. The goal is to get media coverage, which can boost your visibility.

7. **Book Reviews:** Positive reviews can be a powerful tool for marketing your book. Your assistant can send copies of your book to professional reviewers, bloggers, and influencers in your genre.

8. **Book Giveaways:** People love free stuff. Your assistant can run book giveaways on social media or through email. This can help spread the word about your book and attract new readers.

9. **Book Signings and Events:** Even if you can't be there in person, your assistant can represent you at book signings and events. They can sell copies of your book, answer questions, and share your story.

10. **Networking:** Your assistant can help you connect with other authors, publishers, and industry professionals. These relationships can open doors for you and help you reach a wider audience.

Remember, marketing isn't a one-and-done deal. It's an ongoing process, and it takes time and effort to build a readership. But with the right plan and the right assistant, you can get your book the attention it deserves, even from behind bars. After all, your story is too important to keep locked up.

Seizing the Power: Commanding Your Book's Success

To wrap up this chapter on marketing your book, let's reflect on the core message: Even from behind bars, your voice can reach the world. Marketing is about making connections, sparking interest, and stoking the anticipation of your readers. And while the concrete confines may pose some challenges, they also offer unique opportunities for creativity and resilience.

We've covered the importance of understanding your target audience. Remember, your audience is not just any reader, but the readers who will connect with your story, your experiences, and your perspectives. They're the ones who will become your loyal fans, spreading the word about your book and eagerly awaiting your next release.

We've delved into the process of creating a marketing plan. This is a strategic blueprint that will guide you towards your goals. Be clear about what you want to achieve, how much you can invest, the channels you'll use to reach your audience, and the specific tactics that will get you there.

Even without an outside assistant, marketing your book is possible. Building your online presence, leveraging your personal network, participating in online communities, offering free excerpts, and hosting virtual events are all powerful strategies to use. Remember, every tweet, post, or shared excerpt creates a ripple effect that can eventually turn into a wave of interest and sales.

If you have an outside assistant, the marketing world becomes even bigger. A publicist can help amplify your voice, while partnerships with influencers can put your book in front of a whole new audience. Attending book festivals, running promotions, and creating a book trailer are other effective strategies to consider.

But perhaps the most important point to remember is

this: You are not just selling a book; you're sharing a piece of yourself. Your story, your experiences, your unique perspective – that's what readers are really buying. So, pour yourself into your marketing efforts with as much passion and authenticity as you poured into the pages of your book. Your readers will feel that authenticity, and it will resonate with them on a deep level, encouraging them to take a chance on your book.

In the end, marketing is about more than just selling books. It's about establishing a relationship with your readers, telling your story, and making an impact. So, embrace the process, face the challenges head-on, and seize the power to command your book's success.

Building Your Author Platform

> *"If you get eyeballs you'll get engagement."*
> —*Wahida Clark.*

<u>Why Build an Author Platform?</u>

Before delving into the specifics of building an author platform, it is essential to understand why it is important. An *author platform* is a tool that allows you to connect with your readers, build a loyal following, and promote your work. It is a way to establish yourself as an authority in your genre and give readers a reason to seek out your work.

For urban fiction authors, building an author platform is especially important. Urban fiction is a genre that thrives on word-of-mouth promotion and a loyal fan base. By building an author platform, you can create a community of readers who are passionate about your work and who will help spread the word about your books.

Urban and Hip-Hop Magazines: A Bridge to the Incarcerated Community

The roots of urban and hip-hop magazines catering to the black and incarcerated community can be traced back to the civil rights era in the 1960s. Publications like "Ebony" and "Jet" began to highlight the issues, experiences, and triumphs of the black community. The emergence of hip-hop culture in the late 1970s and early 1980s further birthed a new genre of magazines that not only catered to the black community but also mirrored the societal issues, political activism, and cultural expression inherent in hip-hop.

Magazines such as "The Source," "XXL," and "Vibe" played a significant role in shaping the portrayal of black culture and hip-hop. They became a beacon of information for those within and outside the community, including the incarcerated population. Over time, these magazines have provided a unique platform for urban fiction authors to reach a wider audience, including those behind bars.

Esteemed authors like Sister Souljah, Teri Woods, and

K'wan Foye have successfully leveraged this platform to reach the incarcerated community. Their novels, filled with intense, gritty realities and robust, relatable characters, have resonated strongly, leading to a surge in popularity of urban fiction within prison libraries.

Here are some tips for incarcerated aspiring authors to approach these magazines:

1. **Write an Intriguing Query Letter or Proposal.**

Your first point of contact with these magazines will be a query letter or a proposal. This should include a brief introduction about yourself, a summary of your work, and why it will appeal to their readership.

2. **Write and Share Engaging Short Stories or Excerpts.**

If you're able to, write short stories or excerpts from your book and submit them to these magazines. Many magazines have sections dedicated to such submissions, providing an excellent opportunity for exposure.

3. **Leverage the Help of a Trusted Outside Contact.**

Since your ability to access resources might be limited, having a trusted outside contact can be very beneficial. They can help research each magazine's submission guidelines, send your submissions, and follow up on your behalf.

4. **Connect with other Published Authors.**

Writing letters to authors who have successfully published their work in these magazines can provide insight into the process and potentially open doors. Be sure to express genuine admiration for their work and ask for advice or guidance.

5. Be Persistent.

Don't be discouraged by rejection. Keep honing your craft, improving your writing, and persistently reach out to these magazines.

Building relationships with urban and hip-hop magazines offers numerous benefits. Beyond the obvious advantage of reaching a larger audience, it also aids in:

1. Building Credibility.

Being featured in a reputable magazine can significantly enhance your credibility as an author.

2. Opening Doors for Future Opportunities.

Once your work is published in one of these magazines, other opportunities may follow, such as book deals, collaborations with other authors, and even mentoring opportunities.

3. Providing a Platform for Your Voice.

These magazines can provide a platform for sharing your experiences and perspectives, influencing the societal narrative and contributing to the broader conversation about incarceration, rehabilitation, and social justice.

Remember, your voice matters, and your story holds power. Urban and hip-hop magazines cater to a wide and diverse audience eager for authentic, compelling narratives. As an incarcerated author, you bring a unique perspective that can resonate deeply with many readers.

4. Cultivating Empathy and Understanding.

Your stories can help bridge the gap between the incarcerated community and the outside world, fostering empathy, understanding, and potentially sparking dialogue about important issues regarding incarceration and social reform.

5. Developing Personal Growth.

The process of writing, submitting, and engaging with these magazines also contributes to your personal growth. It helps to hone your writing skills, develop resilience, and nurture your ability to communicate effectively.

Conclusion

In conclusion, urban and hip-hop magazines have a rich history of serving as platforms for black culture and the incarcerated community. They provide a unique opportunity for incarcerated authors to share their stories, connect with a larger audience, and contribute to the broader societal conversation. By understanding the landscape, leveraging available resources, and persisting in your efforts, you can successfully build your author platform, even from within your cell. Remember, every great journey begins with a single step, and your first step could be as simple as drafting a letter to one of these magazines. Keep writing, keep sharing, and keep believing in the power of your story.

Urban Fiction Bookclubs

Bookclubs have long been a popular way for readers to come together, discuss literature, and share their love for books. They provide a supportive and engaging environment where readers can explore different genres, discover new authors, and dive deeper into the stories they love. For incarcerated aspiring authors, connecting with bookclubs, especially those focused on Urban Fiction, can be a valuable opportunity to build your author platform and gain exposure for your work.

Understanding Urban Fiction Bookclubs

Urban Fiction Bookclubs specifically focus on books within the urban fiction genre. When approaching Urban Fiction Bookclubs, it's important to familiarize yourself with the genre and its popular authors. This will help you understand the preferences of the bookclub members and engage in meaningful discussions. Here are some tips for approaching Urban Fiction Bookclubs:

1. **Research:** Use the resources available to you, such as books, magazines, or online sources, to research Urban Fiction Bookclubs. Look for clubs that focus on urban fiction or have a diverse reading list that includes the genre. If you have

access to the internet, you can search for online bookclubs as well.

2. **Correspondence:** If you're interested in connecting with a specific bookclub, write a letter expressing your interest in their club and Urban Fiction as a genre. Introduce yourself as an incarcerated aspiring author and offer to contribute to their discussions in any way you can. You can ask a friend or family member on the outside to assist you in finding bookclub contact information and sending the letters.

3. **Book Recommendations:** Suggest your own work or other urban fiction titles that you believe the bookclub members would enjoy. Provide a brief synopsis and explain why you think the book would be a valuable addition to their reading list. If you can, offer to send a copy of your book to the bookclub for their consideration.

Benefits of Urban Fiction Bookclubs

Building relationships with Urban Fiction Bookclubs can have several benefits for incarcerated aspiring authors. Here are a few key advantages:

1. **Feedback and Insights:** Bookclub members can provide valuable feedback and insights into your work. Their discussions can help you understand

how your writing resonates with readers and provide ideas for improvement.

2. **Word-of-Mouth Promotion:** When bookclub members enjoy a book, they often recommend it to others. Positive word-of-mouth can help generate buzz and increase awareness of your work among a wider audience.

3. **Author Visibility:** Participating in bookclub discussions, whether in writing or through audio correspondence, allows you to establish a presence as an author within the Urban Fiction community. This visibility can lead to opportunities for interviews, collaborations, and other promotional activities.

4. **Supportive Community:** Urban Fiction Bookclubs foster a supportive community of readers who are passionate about the genre. Connecting with this community can provide encouragement, motivation, and a network of like-minded individuals who can support your journey as an author.

Remember, when reaching out to bookclubs, be respectful, genuine, and passionate about your work. Engage in meaningful discussions, listen to the perspectives of the bookclub members, and be open to feedback. Building relationships with Urban Fiction Bookclubs can be a powerful way to establish your author platform and connect with readers who share your passion for Urban Fiction. However, it's important to keep in mind the limitations you might face as an incarcerated author. Here are some additional considerations:

1. **Access to Books:** As an incarcerated author, you may have limited access to physical books. However, if you have the ability to receive books from the outside or have access to a prison library, make sure to read widely within the Urban Fiction genre. This will not only enhance your understanding of the genre but also allow you to recommend other books to bookclub members.

2. **Virtual Bookclub Discussions:** If you have access to email or other forms of online communication, you may be able to participate in virtual bookclub discussions. Some bookclubs organize online meetings or have forums where members can discuss the books they're reading. Inquire if the bookclub you're interested in has any virtual options available, and if so, request to join.

3. **Written Contributions:** If you don't have access to online communication, you can still contribute to bookclub discussions through written correspondence. Write thoughtful letters or emails to the bookclub members, sharing your

thoughts on the books they're reading, asking questions, and providing insights from your perspective as an aspiring author. This can create a meaningful dialogue and help you build relationships with the bookclub members.

4. **Engage on Social Media:** Many bookclubs have a presence on social media platforms like Instagram, Twitter, or Facebook. If you have access to these platforms, follow the bookclubs you're interested in and engage with their content. Like, comment, and share their posts, and contribute to discussions around Urban Fiction books. This can help you establish connections and increase your visibility within the bookclub community.

5. **Book Reviews:** Consider writing book reviews of popular Urban Fiction titles and sharing them with the bookclub members. You can write reviews in the form of letters, emails, or even blog posts if you have access to a blogging platform. Sharing your insights and opinions on the books can spark conversations and demonstrate your knowledge of the genre.

Remember, building relationships with Urban Fiction Bookclubs is not just about promoting your own work but also about being an active participant in the community.

Engage in discussions, listen to the perspectives of others, and contribute meaningfully to the bookclub's activities. By doing so, you'll not only establish your author platform but also create lasting connections with readers who share your passion for Urban Fiction. Here are 10 prominent Book Clubs to look into below:

1. Sistah Girls Book Club
2. Queen's Book Club
3. Sip And Flip Book Club
4. My Boozie Book Club
5. BookLIT Book Club
6. Urban Junkie Book Club
7. Hopeful Heartbreakers Book Club
8. Black Girls Read Books, Too (Facebook Group)
9. Bourbon Street Bookers
10. Our Lil' Bookclub (Facebook Group)

Author Podcasts

Podcasts are a prevalent form of new media that has grown immensely popular over the past two decades. The term "podcast" is a portmanteau of "iPod" and "broadcast." It was first coined in the early 2000s as a method to share audio recordings over the internet, taking advantage of the proliferation of portable media devices like Apple's iPod. This concept was not entirely new, as similar forms of audio sharing had been used in previous decades, but the widespread access to the internet and portable digital devices allowed for a much larger audience.

The evolution of podcasting was a boon for content creators and consumers alike. The platform allowed virtually anyone with a microphone and an internet connection to put their voice out into the world. In turn, listeners gained access to a wide variety of content, from educational material to entertainment, that they could consume at their convenience.

As an incarcerated aspiring author, you may wonder how you can leverage the power of podcasts. While you may not be able to start your own podcast from prison, there are other ways you can take advantage of this medium to build your author platform.

Practical Tips

1. **Identifying Podcasts:** First, identify podcasts that align with your writing style, themes, or genre. These could be podcasts that discuss books, author interviews, or topics related to your work. You can do this by asking family members, friends, or your support network on the outside to research suitable podcasts for you.

2. **Outreach:** Once you've identified potential podcasts, the next step is outreach. Write to the podcast hosts or producers, expressing your interest in contributing to their work. You could

offer to share your unique perspective as an incarcerated author, discuss your book, or provide insight into a topic relevant to your writing. Be sure to have a clear and compelling pitch. If you don't have direct access to mail, have someone on the outside assist with this.

3. **Phone Interviews:** Most prisons allow inmates to make phone calls, although there may be restrictions on call length and timing. With the agreement of the podcast host, you could be interviewed over the phone. Although it's not the same as a studio-quality recording, many podcast listeners appreciate authenticity and unique perspectives, and the slight drop in audio quality may not be a significant deterrent.

Benefits of Podcasts

Building relationships with podcast hosts can be a powerful tool for promoting your work and establishing your author platform. Here's why:

1. **Reach a Broad Audience:** Podcasts often have a wide reach, meaning your story could be heard by thousands, if not millions of listeners.

2. **Establish Credibility:** Participating in podcasts can help establish you as a credible author and expert in your genre or field.

3. **Promote Your Book:** Podcasts provide an opportunity to discuss your book and generate interest among potential readers.

4. **Human Connection:** Podcasts are a personal medium, and speaking directly to listeners allows you to connect with them on a human level. This can help build a loyal reader base.

5. **Networking:** Building relationships with podcast hosts can open up other opportunities. Podcast hosts are often well connected and may be able to introduce you to other influencers in your genre or industry.

Conclusion

In conclusion, while there may be barriers to leveraging podcasts as an incarcerated author, the benefits can be significant. With thoughtful planning, a compelling pitch, and the assistance of your support network on the outside, you can make the most of this powerful platform.

Overcoming Challenges

There may be challenges you will face as an incarcerated author trying to make an appearance on a podcast. However, don't let this deter you. Here's how you can overcome them:

1. **Limited Call Time:** If your prison restricts the length of phone calls, this could limit the length of your podcast interview. To overcome this, you

could arrange with the host to have multiple sessions or prepare your thoughts in advance to make the most of the time you have.

2. **Call Quality:** The audio quality on prison phone lines may not be the best. Podcast hosts and listeners are generally understanding and appreciative of unique voices and perspectives, so this may not be a major issue. In your pitch to the podcast host, make sure to let them know of this limitation.

3. **Limited Research Capabilities:** You might not be able to listen to the show before your interview or have limited context about the host and previous episodes. In this case, rely on your support network on the outside to provide you with information and context about the podcast.

4. **Security Protocols:** Each prison has different rules around phone calls. You might need to get clearance from the prison to make these calls. Be sure to understand and follow all the rules.

Remember, the most important thing is to share your unique story and perspective. Podcasts offer an intimate way to connect with potential readers and other authors. It's an opportunity to let your voice be heard, even from within the confines of a prison cell. So, don't let the challenges deter you from utilizing this platform.

The Role of Social Media

Social media is a powerful tool for building an author platform, and it is particularly important for authors who are incarcerated. Social media allows you to reach a wide audience, connect with readers and industry professionals, and promote your work.

As an Urban Fiction author, you should focus on using social media platforms that are popular with your target audience. Platforms like Instagram, Twitter, and Facebook can be effective tools for promoting your work and building your author platform.

When using social media, it is important to be authentic and engaging. Share snippets of your writing, behind-the-scenes glimpses into your life, and insights into your creative process. Respond to comments and messages from your followers and use social media to build a community of readers who are passionate about your work.

Black Bookstagram

The "Black Bookstagram" community, as we know it today, began to truly coalesce around 2016. It was a response to the longstanding issue of underrepresentation of Black authors and narratives within the broader literary community. The term "Bookstagram" is a portmanteau of "book" and "Instagram," and it refers to the community of book lovers who share their reading interests, book reviews, and stylized photos of books on Instagram. Black Bookstagram specifically focuses on promoting and supporting Black authors and stories.

The emergence of the Black Bookstagram community is closely tied to the rise of social media, which has allowed individuals worldwide to connect and share their experiences. By leveraging this widespread, easily accessible platform, Black Bookstagrammers have been able to highlight works by Black authors, promote conversations around these books, and provide a richer context for understanding and appreciating them.

Approaching the Black Bookstagram Community

1. **Identify Your Advocates:** You'll need someone on the outside who has access to the internet and can help manage your online presence. This could be a friend, family member, or even a fellow writer who believes in your work and is willing to help build your platform.

2. **Create Quality Content:** Your advocate can help share your story, your journey as a writer in prison, and insights about your book. High-quality content is key, as it can help generate interest in you and your work. This could include excerpts from your book, your writing process, or your experiences as an incarcerated individual.

3. **Engage with the Community:** Encourage your advocate to engage with other Black

Bookstagrammers. This might mean commenting on their posts, sharing their content, or starting a conversation about books they've recommended. Genuine engagement is crucial to building relationships within this community.

4. **Be Authentic:** Authenticity resonates with people. Share your struggles, victories, hopes, and fears. Let your voice be heard through your words. This will not only make you relatable but also create a strong connection with your readers.

Benefits of Building Relationships with the Black Bookstagram Community

1. **Increased Visibility:** The Black Bookstagram community is highly active and influential. Having your work shared by a Black Bookstagrammer can significantly increase your visibility among readers who may be interested in your book.

2. **Feedback and Support:** Black Bookstagrammers are avid readers who can provide valuable feedback on your work. They can also offer support and encouragement, which can be especially valuable in a prison environment.

3. **Networking Opportunities:** Building relationships with Black Bookstagrammers can

open doors to other networking opportunities. You may be introduced to publishers, agents, writers, or other relevant contacts in the literary field.

4. **Creating a Legacy:** By contributing to the Black Bookstagram community, you're playing a part in the larger movement to diversify the literary world. Your unique perspective as an incarcerated author can add to the richness of the stories shared within the community.

Remember, patience is key in building these relationships. It might take time, but a strong, authentic connection with the Black Bookstagram community can provide a solid foundation for your author platform and profoundly impact your writing journey. I have to warn you, though. Like all avenues, there are people who will get into something just to make money or as a hobby thing but they're not really business oriented. They play with your money, handle business on their time the way they want, run off with your check, promise you things and fail to come through, mispronounce your book and/or company name, their content is blurry and unprofessional, I can go on and on. Here are 10 Bookstagrammers listed below that I have used personally that handle AI business. Some of them may be a lil on the expensive side, some just want a free copy of your book, and some are free. Have your people reach out to them:

1. @chocolatecoveredpages
2. @shangeereads
3. @readnliftwithshar
4. @melanatedreader
5. @bdmreads
6. @booksandsou1ı
7. @babes_readbooks
8. @brwnsugarreads
9. @blkbookaddict
10. @keysbookshelf_

Networking

Networking is another important tool for building an author platform. While networking may be more challenging for authors who are incarcerated, it is still possible to make connections and build relationships with industry professionals.

One way to network is to attend writing conferences and events. While you may not be able to physically attend these events, many conferences and events now offer virtual participation options. Take advantage of these opportunities to connect with other writers and industry professionals and to learn more about the publishing industry.

Another way to network is to join writing organizations and groups. These groups can be found online and can provide valuable resources and support for authors. They can also be a great way to connect with other writers who share your interests and goals.

Finally, it is important to remember that networking is a two-way street. Be willing to help others, share your knowledge and expertise, and be open to opportunities that may come your way.

Apart from joining writing organizations and attending virtual events, building relationships with other incarcerated authors can be a potent networking tool. This community shares a unique set of experiences and can offer invaluable insights, support, and collaboration opportunities. By exchanging letters, manuscripts, or critiques, you can significantly broaden your perspectives, enrich your own work, and foster a sense of camaraderie.

Magazines and publications, particularly those focusing on prisoner writings, are another valuable networking resource. For instance, penning articles, stories, or poems for these platforms not only helps you gain visibility but also helps you connect with the editors, readers, and other contributing authors. To get started, you could request friends, family, or legal representatives outside to help research such publications and initiate the process of submission.

Blogs and catalogs that feature prison literature can also be of significant benefit. While direct online interaction might not be feasible, having someone outside who can manage your digital presence can be an effective work-around. They can submit your writings, relay any responses, and help you establish an online footprint. It's important to note that this should be done in accordance with the prison's rules and regulations.

Creating a newsletter or a zine is another excellent way of networking. This can be circulated within the prison or, with the right assistance, to other prisons as well. This can be an avenue for sharing your work, promoting the work of others, or discussing the challenges and triumphs of writing from within prison walls.

Lastly, remember that networking is not just about gaining, it's about giving as well. Share your knowledge, experiences, and skills freely. Offer constructive critique on others' works, help newcomers navigate the literary landscape, and offer encouragement. Networking is about building relationships, and relationships are built on mutual assistance, respect, and understanding.

Networking from prison might present unique challenges, but remember, it is not only possible but also potentially rewarding. The key is to be persistent, creative, and supportive of others in the community.

Conclusion

In conclusion, building an author platform as an urban fiction author from prison requires dedication, perseverance, and a willingness to learn and adapt. By leveraging the power of social media, networking, and self-publishing, you can establish yourself as an authority in your genre and create a loyal following of readers.

Remember to focus on creating high-quality content, engaging with your audience, and building meaningful relationships with industry professionals. With hard work and persistence, you can build a successful author platform and achieve your goals as an author.

CHAPTER 10

Overcoming Obstacles

[On her jail time]: "I can't say it was negative. Without it there is
no way I would've written a book."
—Wahida Clark

Writing From Behind Bars

When Wahida Clark entered the women's federal penitentiary in Lexington, Kentucky, Dickens, her husband, was
just finishing his prison term. She hadn't been able to return
home to get the family affairs in order. One day, she called to
get money for her commissary account, but her family told
her there was nothing to give. All of their businesses were
gone. All of the money was gone. The cars were being repos-

sessed and the house was in foreclosure. They had even pawned her Rolex watch for $50. Wahida worked in the library at prison and taught computer classes, but she knew she needed more money. She hung up the phone and started to pray, wondering what she was going to do to make money while in prison. Her kids were on the outside and she had to take care of them. Her husband was locked up and she needed to send him money. Very shortly after that, she received her answer.

"Prison jobs in federal prisons usually pay 25 cents to $1 per hour," said Lauren-Brooke Eisen, director, Justice Program at the Brennan Center for Justice at NYU School of Law. Any money inmates do make can be directed to paying court fees, restitution or the cost of incarceration. *"For the vast majority of people behind bars, there is no way to provide for their families,"* Eisen said. But Wahida became an outlier, one of a small groups of inmates who would take their experiences, real or fictionalized, and turn a profit by **writing about them from behind bars.**

In 2016, Curtis Dawkins, who is serving a life sentence in Michigan for murdering a man during a botched robbery, scored a book deal with Simon and Schuster for $150,000. Two years later, the state wanted him to redirect 90% of his assets from an education fund for his three children to state coffers to pay for cost of his imprisonment, according to a report in The New York Times. But before Dawkins was an inmate, he earned a masters of fine arts degree. Wahida, like most other inmates writing in the street lit genre, had no such training.

Her turning point was seeing a magazine story about Shannon Holmes, a pioneer of modern street lit who had no prior writing experience, write a book while in prison. Wahida began to envision her own name on the spines of books in the library. She told her husband, and he told her that if she was going to write a book, the only thing they're buying from us is books about pimping, hoeing, and drugs.

She came up with a storyline, a tale of three women choosing between the thugs they love or a life beyond crime and wrote every day in longhand on a yellow legal pad. She signed up for a creative writing class and started reading urban literature. In six months, Wahida had the makings of a novel. She wrote to Carl Weber, a popular African American author at the time, for advice on getting published. Weber wrote back and told her he was starting a publishing company.

"That was when I got my first book deal," Wahida said. She had family members type her manuscript, and she asked prison staff to help her get it copied. *"When the book was published in 2002, 15 copies arrived at the prison, but the check for $25,000 in royalties bounced and the company went out of business,"* she said. Not exactly sure how true this is, but an AJC article stated that Carl Weber did not respond to a request for comment on the deal.

Despite Wahida not receiving that money, the prison

lieutenant took notice of Wahida's burgeoning success. She was summoned to the office and grilled on how she managed to publish a book while in jail and ended up in solitary confinement. *"They said I was there for writing a book and profiting from it when the prison says you are not supposed to do that,"* she said.

"Most people behind bars are not getting book deals, so policies can vary from one prison to the next," said experts. *"The few situations where someone had a source of income that was significant that was not part of the prison economy, those are taken on a case-by-case basis,"* Eisen said. During nine months spent in solitary confinement, Wahida started writing what would become her second book series. When she was transferred to Alderson, the minimum-security women's prison in West Virginia, she got an agent, a new book deal, an advance from Kensington Publishing Corp., and the rest was history.

In any journey, the path is seldom smooth. In the journey of writing and publishing a book, this is as true as ever, and the barriers you face may seem even more formidable from within the walls of a prison. But remember this: every obstacle is a stepping stone, and every challenge an opportunity for growth.

1. Harnessing the Power of Perspective.

The first obstacle in your journey may well be your own perspective. You may feel that your current circumstances hinder your ability to write and publish your work. However, this need not be the case. It's essential to shift your perspective and see your situation not as a cage, but as a *transformative experience* through which you could come into a new or altered sense of identity. Prisons have housed many great authors over the years, from Dutch to CA$H, and even Mike Enemigo who have turned their experiences into profound literary works. You, too, can channel your experiences and emotions into your writing, enriching it with a depth and authenticity that only lived experience can provide.

1. Time – A Gift, Not an Obstacle.

From an outside perspective, it may seem like time is against you. That's not true. While your days may have a strict routine, you also have something many aspiring authors lack, *uninterrupted time*. Use this to your advantage. Make writing a part of your routine. Capture thoughts, feelings, and observations as they come. Over time, these snippets of life can evolve into a compelling narrative.

1. Overcoming Limited Resources.

Access to resources can be an obstacle, but it is not insurmountable. Books, paper, pens — these may be more difficult to come by, but they are not impossible to find. Reach out to prison library staff or educators, as they may be able to help you secure the tools you need.

Moreover, never underestimate the power of your mind, your memory, and your ability to create. JK Rowling began the Harry Potter series on a delayed train journey without a pen, merely visualizing the world and characters in her mind. You, too, can start your story within the landscape of your imagination.

1. Dealing with Isolation and Loneliness.

Isolation can be both an obstacle and a tool. It's natural to feel lonely and cut off from the world, but remember, writing has been a solace to many in isolation. It can be a way for you to connect with your inner self and the world outside. Your words can bridge distances, reach hearts, and resonate in the souls of readers you may never meet.

1. The Fear of Rejection.

Fear of rejection is an obstacle all authors, regardless of their circumstances, must face. Your unique situation may intensify this fear but remember that rejection is *a part* of the process, not the end of it. Every rejection is a step closer to acceptance. It's an opportunity to learn, improve, and grow.

<u>Final Thoughts</u>

Above all, remember that your voice matters. Your story is unique and valuable, and it deserves to be shared with the world. You may be incarcerated, but ***your mind is free***. With persistence, resilience, and belief in yourself, you can overcome the obstacles in your path and achieve your dream of publishing a book.

Remember, your current situation is not your final destination. You are *a writer*. You *are a storyteller*. And the world is waiting to hear *your story*.

EXAMPLE DOCUMENTS

I decided to put this section together to give you a few examples of the things that were mentioned in this book, things that I had to have my people print off the Internet and mail in to me. I racked my brain thinking of things that I may have forgotten to mention, but only came up with examples. I understand that for some of you this whole process is foreign but I also know that it will begin to make sense the more diligent that you are and the more you learn. So here are a few things I figured I should touch basis on:

- <u>**Synopsis Writing**</u>

  Since becoming a publisher, one of the things I noticed is that a lot of people have no idea how to write a synopsis and some don't even know what a synopsis is.

A *synopsis* is a 500-800 word summary of your book that forms part of your agent submission pack. It should outline your plot in neutral non-salesy language and demonstrate a clear narrative arc. Every character, any big turning point or climactic scene, and all plot twists should get a mention.

Below is the synopsis for my book *Triggadale: Shots Fired.* Use it as an example of how to structure a synopsis and what one is supposed to look like when sending it in with your submission:

Triggadale Synopsis:

It's "gunz-up" in Riverdale. A trigger-happy youngin' becomes the target of retribution when he murders the twin brother of a well-respected gang member in his quest to establish his crew as the dominating force of the Southside.

DALDRICK BLANDING (HUNCHO), rambunctious street nigga and prominent member of Southside Mafia, ignites a war that sets off a trail of bloodfire across Clayton County, making him the target of two unrelenting foes: a vengeful brother and an ambitious justice-seeking detective. A Grove St. vet, DEANDRE CHAMBERS (DRE) is a major face in the infamous Hit Squad Taliban. Tragically, his twin brother is murdered right before his eyes by none other than Huncho himself. Dre, a certified hitta, vows to claim his life and the live of any and all associated with him. However, the beef has made both sides the target of Georgia Gang Act Laws; they are primary targets of a Special Task force.

Seeking the demise of both sides is DETECTIVE BRIAN ELLIS, the former Navy Seal and Gang Task volunteer. He sees the Gang crisis as an opportunity to advance within the law enforcement infrastructure. A major take down would increase his chances at being promoted to Chief of Police. When it comes to the vast numbers of bodies turning up all over Clayton County, there's no doubt in his mind that Huncho and Dre are behind the majority. All he needs is a witness.

Triggadale opens at a Saturday night club scene. In which Huncho murders Taliban (Dre's twin brother) in cold blood after Hit Squad brutally assaults his homeboy Nard. As Dre helplessly held his brother in his arms as he died, he vowed to avenge him even if it meant he must take off Mafiosos one by one until he gets to Huncho.

Several incidents follow, arrests are made, and a Special Task Force is put together to bring the senseless madness to an end. Huncho, who had been brought up by several arrested affiliates as Taliban's suspected murderer, is now a suspect. At a Task Force briefing, Detective Brian Ellis (Head of Operations) is asked his opinion of the validity of these statements, but due to them all being second-hand, he stresses the importance of a witness with a first-hand account.

Dre gets the drop on Huncho at a football game; he damn near makes good on his oath, aiming for his head but by default, hits him in the neck. The bullet ends up going straight through.

FLAME, Huncho's right-hand-man, puts some female MAFIOSOS (Southside Queens) on TEVO, Dre's closest friend/Frontline H.S.T affiliate. Not long after Huncho's release from the hospital, Reka (a Queen) sets Tevo up to get jumped. However, he, instead, gets killed.

The media coverage of Tevo's murder brings the heat down on the Special Task Force; Detective Ellis is forced to round up members on both sides. Witness fishing, he uses Georgia Gang Act Laws to hold validated affiliates without cause for seventy-two hours, but gains nothing for his troubles.

News of Tevo's murder reaches Reka, who had previous relations with him in her younger years, and her weight of her guilt drives her to attend his funeral. There, she is recognized by females from Grove St. as a Queen; also as the last one to see Tevo alive by Hit Squad. Subsequently, she's murdered.

As a result, Southside Queens pop on some females from Grove St. The brawl ends with Yana (a Queen) unable to flee the scene, getting arrested "red-handed" directly after shooting SHEA (a squad affiliate). Ellis interrogates her, and under pressure, she reveals that she was Huncho's getaway driver the night he killed Taliban.

With Yana as state's witness, Huncho and Flame rob a dopeman for "fugitive funds" and flee to Alabama, where they set up shop. Huncho has Yana killed, while out on bond and instructs the Queens to get in good with Dre.

Realizing they may need lawyer fare, Huncho and Dre plan a trip back to Riverdale to re-up and drop money off to their mothers. While they are at it, they put an end to Dre once and for all. They return to Riverdale, deliver lawyer fare to their mothers, re-up with PURP (a major character in *Triggadale's* sequel), then set off to handle Dre.

The showdown is *Triggadale's* climax, in which Southside Queens succeed in giving Huncho and Flame the element of surprise. Gotti (a squad affiliate) is killed by Flame. Flame is then gunned down by police after opening fire on them. Meanwhile, Dre and Huncho standoff gun-to-gun). Dre is killed by backup officers as he flees from the scene; Huncho barely escapes capture by law enforcement officials.

GBI hot on his tail, he returns to Alabama but is tracked down through cell phone records of calls to an Alabama native (Huncho's country fling, Monica). In desperation, he takes her hostage, and finds himself at a standoff with the law. Detective Ellis is brought in to negotiate his surrender, and Huncho seemingly relents. He releases Monica, but when Ellis approaches, he unloads the choppa on him; he is gunned down himself by S.W.A.T Team officers.

Huncho is awaken by Corrections Officers. He's in chain-gang (with Life plus five for murdering Taliban), where he's been for the last three years. Everything after the showdown had been a dream (backfill done in story). He made it off the scene but passed out in a barn in Fayetteville. Discovered by an old lady the following morning, he was turned in. The Corrections Officer is at Huncho's door to escort him to transport. He's going back for his appeal, setting the stage for "Triggadale II".

• <u>Back Cover Book Blurb</u>

A ***back cover blurb*** offers a snapshot of the book and sparks curiosity. It should address the central topics or themes without being too vague, clever, or flashy. Keep it short. A fiction blurb for adult readers should be 175 – 225 words.

Many people mistakenly call this the synopsis, but it's not. Many authors write these and erroneously submit this with their manuscript. The problem is, the description is too vague for publishers and Beta readers to decide if it will be a good fit for the company. So, unless the sample chapters are just *that* good, it may be the cause of you not receiving a response.

Below is the back cover book blurb of *Stuck In The Trenches: Welcome To The District of Columbia* by Huff Tha Great. This is an example of what one is supposed to look like. You may structure it different but hopefully, this gives you an idea of what you're setting out to put together.

Back Cover Book Blurb

After witnessing his father's death, 18-year-old Trey Johnson wholeheartedly lives up to his nickname Young Savage, alongside his best friend in the game, 23-year-old Damian aka Freaky. Keeping his head on a swivel, bands in his pockets, and a dog on him at all times, Savage has no remorse in hitting a lick and committing murder if needed. With money on his mind and plenty of women in his bed, he is living his best life while surviving the mean streets of D.C. the best way he knows how.

However, unbeknownst to him, Savage's life becomes a hot commodity when revenge is the motive. One lick has fatal consequences, and payback instantly becomes a top priority. Before his death, Big Savage taught Savage to always be aware of his surroundings. While dealing with an unwanted distraction, will Savage get caught slipping and revenge be served? Or will Savage be the one delivering his own brand of justice?

Take a ride through the District of Columbia with Young Savage and find out what type of thoroughbreds those streets breed. See what happens when the right amount of pressure is applied, and what these grimy streets turn the real ones into. It's a test to see if Savage is built to survive the trenches with snakes lurking in the grass or will he become prey, left to be eaten alive and swallowed up like so many before him.

- <u>**Cover Letter Template**</u>

Publishers and many literary agents require a cover letter along with your sample chapters and synopsis. This is a formal introduction to you and your novel:

[Your Name]
    [Your Address]
    [City, State, Zip Code]
    [Email Address]
    [Phone Number]
    [Date]

[Publisher's Name or Editor's Name]
    [Publisher's Company]
    [Company Address]
    [City, State, Zip Code]

Dear [Publisher's Name or Editor's Name],

I hope this letter finds you well. I am writing to present my manuscript entitled "Whispers of the Ancients," a work of historical fantasy that I believe would be a compelling addition to [Publisher's Company]'s catalogue, particularly given your reputation for publishing engaging and imaginative narratives.

The story unfolds across 450 pages and is set in a world

where the boundaries between myth and reality blur. "Whispers of the Ancients" transports readers to an era where the remnants of old powers linger in the shadows, waiting to be awakened by the descendants of a forgotten lineage. It follows the journey of Elara, a young herbalist who discovers her connection to a secret society that has safeguarded the world from untold darkness. As she delves deeper into her ancestry, Elara must navigate the treacherous political landscape of her time while mastering the ancient magic that flows through her veins.

My inspiration for this manuscript stems from a deep appreciation for history and mythology, combined with a desire to explore the themes of legacy, identity, and the human connection to the natural world. I have dedicated two years to the research and writing of this novel, ensuring that every detail enriches the narrative and resonates with the reader.

I have previously published short stories in [Magazine/Journal Name(s)], which have been well received by readers and have helped me hone my craft. The manuscript of "Whispers of the Ancients" has been professionally edited and is ready for publication.

I am aware of [Publisher's Company]'s success in launching the careers of fantasy authors and am enthusiastic about the possibility of partnering with you. I believe that my novel's blend of historical intrigue and magical realism will appeal to your audience and fits seamlessly within the genre you so expertly represent.

Enclosed, please find the first three chapters and a synopsis of "Whispers of the Ancients." I am prepared to send the complete manuscript at your request. I would be thrilled to discuss the potential for collaboration further and am open to any feedback you might have.

Thank you for considering my submission. I look forward to the opportunity to work with [Publisher's Company] and am excited about the possibility of seeing my work in print under your esteemed imprint.

Warm regards,

[Your Name]

[Enclosures: First Three Chapters, Synopsis]

- ## Story Outline

A *story outline* is a structured plan that guides you as you write your manuscripts. It typically includes a summary of the major events of the plot, the main characters and their motivations, the setting, and any other main themes or ideas that the story explores. Below is an example of what one is supposed to look like. I used *Wet Dreams On Lockdown: The Female C.O by Telia Teanna for this one*. Again, you may structure it different but hopefully this gives you an idea of what you're setting out to put together.

Wet Dreams On Lockdown: The Female C.O Outline

Chapter One: Zyan is frustrated when he's attempting to call his girlfriend McKenzie and she doesn't answer. Stressed, he decides to blow steam, watch porn, and masturbate. While doing the do, a female officer comes in, interrupting him. She's dropping a pack for his celly, Pressure. They have a brief exchange, she leaves, and his interest is peaked.

Sulani is leaving her shift when she sees Dolo, her ex and co-worker, waiting for her at her car and sighs. He's upset about the fact that she switched shifts to avoid being around him. The two are on bad terms and have an argument about their recent break up. Once she makes it home, she showers, masturbates to porn and thoughts of Zyan and what he was doing when she had walked into his cell earlier. Later, she makes a call to her cousin, Gemini, to get some info on Zyan.

Chapter Two: Sulani arrives at her shift and she's in the staff break room to get some coffee when another officer, one she had a negative experience with when he tried to force himself on her, causing Dolo to beat him up. He taunts her and she ignores his banter and leaves. She's sitting at her desk when Zyan approaches the door and starts talking to her. She entertains him briefly but is slightly irate because she doesn't like to be approached when she's working because of Dolo. People are always watching her and reporting her every move to him. She tells him she will tell Pressure to give Zyan her number and he could contact her that way.

Later the two are having a text exchange when Sulani begins getting aroused at the conversation and throws caution to the wind and goes up to his cell where she has sex with Zyan and sucks Pressure off. She leaves satisfied.

Chapter Three: Zyan and Pressure have a discussion about how Pressure knows Sulani and mentions they seemed very comfortable with being intimate with one another. Pressure shares that she's the cousin of his girlfriend, Gemini, and that they are good friends. They are talking when McKenzie is mentioned, and Zyan has a flashback to the day that his mother kicked him out of their family home and he met McKenzie. Pressure gives him some advice to ease up on McKenzie, and he receives it and decides he needs a distraction when he gets a text from Sulani with a picture. Just the distraction that he needed.

Zyan and Pressure are coming in from yard when they are approached by Dolo and two other officers. Dolo orders the two to get on their knees and put their hands behind their backs. Zyan is combative and refusing and Pressure convinces him to listen and not make it worse than it needs to be. They are ushered to the back where Dolo tells him to stay away from Sulani and Zyan and Pressure mock him and his backup. While they laugh, Dolo attacks and Zyan dodges him. A fight ensues and the two inmates fight the officers until Zyan gets knocked out, and Pressure is tazed.

Chapter Four: Zyan texts Sulani and tells her he fought her boyfriend. They have a back and forth until Zyan gives her a call and they have a discussion about Sulani's relationship with her ex, Pressure, and their threesome. The calls ends with them about to have phone sex.

Sulani is at home relaxing when Dolo breaks into her house drunk and they have a scuffle. The cops are called, Dolo goes to jail, and Sulani is rattled. After getting settled, she calls Zyan and he comforts her. She opens up about how much of a wakeup call things were.

Chapter Five: Sulani is having a threesome with Zyan and Pressure. Pressure is getting ready to be released and they are "celebrating." She's living her best life.

Gemini gives her cousin a call and the two of them gossip and talk about the threesome and that she was glad that she had fun even though she was fucking her man.

Sulani and Zyan are having an intimate conversation, and she apologizes to Zyan for putting him at risk. The two come to an understanding that they are friends with benefits and looking forward to seeing where things go between the two of them.

The story closes with them indulging in highly anticipated and needed sex.

• **Magazine Query Letter Template**

A *magazine query letter* is more than a pitch. A pitch in a query letter equates to the first paragraph. Yet, it's the whole letter that sells the article or story idea. Much like a book proposal, a query letter for a publication of any type serves as a marketing document. Here's an example / template of one below:

Subject: Query: Celebrating the Pulse of the City through Vibrant Storytelling

Dear [Editor's Name],

I hope this message finds you well. My name is [Your Full Name], and I'm a writer and cultural enthusiast with a deep appreciation for the richness of urban life and the dynamic tapestry that is the African American experience. As a regular reader of [Magazine's Name], I've been continually inspired by your commitment to stories that resonate with authenticity and pulse with the vibrant heartbeats of our communities.

I'm reaching out to propose a feature article that I believe will align perfectly with the editorial vision of [Magazine's Name]. The working title is "[Article Title]: [Subtitle]" and it intends to explore [briefly describe the central theme or subject of your article].

Here's why I think this story will captivate your readers:
- Reason 1: Perhaps it's a fresh angle on a familiar topic, or

it addresses an issue that's currently trending in the black urban community.

- Reason 2: Explain how your article will provide value to readers, such as practical advice, inspiration, or deep insights into a cultural phenomenon.

- Reason 3: Describe the unique elements you bring to the table, like exclusive interviews, personal narratives, or expert commentary.

My previous work has been featured in [Mention any notable publications, if applicable], and I've honed my voice to speak to issues that matter to our community with both nuance and vigor. [If you have any relevant qualifications or experiences, briefly note them here.]

I envision this piece being approximately [word count] words and would be excited to submit it for your consideration on [specific time frame]. Should you be interested, I'd be happy to provide a detailed outline along with a sample of my writing.

I believe that [Article Title] will not only engage your audience but also spark important conversations that affirm the spirit and diversity of the black urban experience. I am eager to contribute to the powerful dialogue that [Magazine's Name] fosters.

Thank you for considering my proposal. I look forward to the possibility of working together to celebrate and elevate the stories that shape our world.

Warm regards,

[Your Full Name]

[Your Contact Information]

[Links to your writing portfolio or social media, if applicable]

P.S. [Optional: Add a postscript if there's a timely hook or any additional information that could sway the editor's interest in your pitch.]

ASSISTED PUBLISHING PACKAGES

Bronze Package $400

Cover

Editing

Formatting

Silver Package $725

Cover

Editing

Formatting

1 Flyer

Typing

Gold Package $975

Cover

Editing

Formatting

2 Flyers

Typing

Proofreading

Copyright Registration

Upload Book To Amazon

Platinum Package $1,200

Everything in the Bronze, Silver & Gold Package

An additional flyer

Set up Amazon Account

1 Month Book Promotion on FB & IG

AUTHOR'S NOTE

Thank you for taking the time to read my guide. I hope it helps you tremendously as you enter the world of writing and publishing. I plan to continue this journey with more "How To From Prison Books," providing you with valuable insights and guidance from my own experiences. If this book has been helpful to you in any way, please support me by requesting URBAN AINT DEAD books from Sure Shot Books, Special Needs X-Press, the catalogs you order books from, and prison libraries. Additionally, encourage your family and friends to purchase from our website, where they can also book a consultation to get answers to any questions they may have.

Furthermore, if you're seeking a comprehensive resource of companies that cater specifically to prisoners, I highly recommend Mike Enemigo's "The Best Resource Directory

For Prisoners." This book is an excellent tool, and they regularly update it to ensure the information remains current. Make sure you're ordering the latest edition to have access to the most accurate and up-to-date resources available.

Your support means the world to me, and I am committed to continuing to provide valuable content and resources to help you succeed. With that said, make sure you check out the Example Document section at the end for more helpful information, and thank you once again. I look forward to connecting with you through future publications and consultations.

ABOUT THE AUTHOR

<u>**Elijah R. Freeman**</u> is an author from Riverdale, Georgia, and a two-time UBAWA Top 100 Author's award winner. Having penned 10 novels so far, he is quickly becoming known as "The Future of Urban Fiction". He is now the C.E.O. of URBAN AINT DEAD and has made some of the biggest moves from behind the wall. His books have appeared in KITE Magazine, States Vs. Us, Prison Legal News and Aspiring Authors Magazine.

Did you enjoy the read?

Let us know how much by leaving us a review on Amazon and Goodreads.

OTHER BOOKS BY

URBAN AINT DEAD

Tales 4rm Da Dale

The Hottest Summer Ever

Hittin' Licks For The Holidays: Atlanta

Wet Dreams On Lockdown: The Nurse

By **Elijah R. Freeman**

Despite The Odds

By **Juhnell Morgan**

Good Girls Gone Rogue

Good Girls Gone Rouge 2

By **Manny Black**

Hittaz

Hittaz 2

Hittaz 3

Hittaz 4

Coldhearted

By **Lou Garden Price, Sr.**

Charge It To The Game

Charge It To The Game 2

A Summer To Remember With My Hitta

Snatched Up By A Hitta

Santa Sent Me A Real One For Christmas

Wet Dreams on Lockdown: The Unit Manager

Thug Me The Right Way 2

Thug Me The Right Way 3

By **Nai**

A Setup For Revenge

Wet Dreams On Lockdown: The Librarian

By **Ashley Williams**

Ridin' For You

Ridin' For You, Too

Trickin' on a Heaux for Christmas: A BBW Love Story

Homie Hoppin' For The Holidays

Wet Dreams on Lockdown: The Female C.O

By **Telia Teanna**

The State's Witness

The State's Witness 2

The State's Witness 3

This Time Won't You Save Me

By **Kyiris Ashley**

Stuck In The Trenches

Stuck In The Trenches 2

By **Huff Tha Great**

The Swipe

By **Toōla**

Melted the Heart of a Menace

Wet Dreams On Lockdown: Lieutenant Grace

By P. Wise

Merry Trapmas: Ice & Frost

By **Mia Sky**

Thug Me The Right Way

By **DiamondATL & Nai**

Atlantastan

By **Chris Green**

Wet Dreams on Lockdown: The Male C.O

By **Tamyra Griffin**

Wet Dreams On Lockdown: The Counselor

By **Paris Iman**

Wet Dreams On Lockdown: The Warden

By **Shawnice**

Wet Dreams On Lockdown: The Captain

By **TN Jones**

COMING SOON FROM
URBAN AINT DEAD

The Hottest Summer Ever 2
THE G-CODE
Tales 4rm Da Dale 2
By **Elijah R. Freeman**

Hittaz 5
Coldhearted 2
By **Lou Garden Price, Sr.**

The Swipe 2
By **Toola**

Good Girl Gone Rogue 3
By **Manny Black**

Despite The Odds 2
Hittin' Licks For The Holidays: Chicago
By **Juhnell Morgan**

Charge It To The Game 3
By **Nai**

A Setup For Revenge 2
By **Ashley Williams**

This Time Won't You Save Me 2
By **Kyiris Ashley**

Ridin' For You 3
By **Telia Teanna**

A Gangsta's Last Kiss
By **Mia Sky**

Pretti & The Beast
By **P. Wise**

BOOKS BY

URBAN AINT DEAD's C.E.O

Elijah R. Freeman

Triggadale

Triggadale 2

Triggadale 3

Tales 4rm Da Dale

The Hottest Summer Ever

Murda Was The Case

Murda Was The Case 2

Murda Was The Case 3

Hittin' Licks For The Holidays: Atlanta

Wet Dreams On Lockdown: The Nurse

STAY CONNECTED

Follow
Elijah R. Freeman
On Social Media
FB: Elijah R. Freeman
IG: @the_future_of_urban_fiction